Time Management

Simple Strategies to Maximize Productivity

*(Increase Your Productivity, Reduce Your Stress,
and Improve Your Work-life Balance)*

Anthony Braden

Published By **Jordan Levy**

Anthony Braden

All Rights Reserved

Time Management: Simple Strategies to Maximize Productivity (Increase Your Productivity, Reduce Your Stress, and Improve Your Work-life Balance)

ISBN 978-1-9992226-4-2

No part of this guidebook shall be reproduced in any form without permission in writing from the publisher except in the case of brief quotations embodied in critical articles or reviews.

Legal & Disclaimer

The information contained in this book is not designed to replace or take the place of any form of medicine or professional medical advice. The information in this book has been provided for educational & entertainment purposes only.

The information contained in this book has been compiled from sources deemed reliable, and it is accurate to the best of the Author's knowledge; however, the Author cannot guarantee its accuracy and validity and cannot be held liable for any errors or omissions. Changes are periodically made to this book. You must consult your doctor or get professional medical advice before using any of the suggested remedies, techniques, or information in this book.

Upon using the information contained in this book, you agree to hold harmless the Author from and against any damages, costs, and expenses, including any legal fees potentially resulting from the application of any of the information provided by this guide. This disclaimer applies to any damages or injury caused by the use and application, whether directly or indirectly, of any advice or information presented, whether for breach of contract, tort, negligence, personal injury, criminal intent, or under any other cause of action.

You agree to accept all risks of using the information presented inside this book. You need to consult a professional medical practitioner in order to ensure you are both able and healthy enough to participate in this program.

Table Of Contents

Chapter 1: Importance Of Time Management

Importance of Self-Assessment

Self-assessment is a important and often overlooked step in powerful time manage. Many humans start organizing their time without first actually information how they will be presently spending their hours. The self-evaluation offers a strong basis to begin enhancing time manipulate via way of imparting an correct and unique information of the manner time is being used.

As with any adventure, we need a starting point, an area from which to start our route to improvement. That is exactly what the self-evaluation gives: a properly-described place to begin.

Self-assessment additionally performs a critical function in identifying time-use patterns and conduct. These patterns, as quickly as diagnosed, may be analyzed to decide whether or no longer they'll be useful or damaging to productiveness. For instance, you could find through self-assessment which you are more green within the morning or that sure sports have a tendency to take longer than predicted. These findings are beneficial even as planning and placing time manage dreams.

Additionally, self-assessment can provide insight into your values and priorities. The manner we spend our time is, in plenty of techniques, a pondered picture of what we charge. If you spend an lousy lot of a while jogging, you can price profession and profession achievement. If you spend a outstanding deal of time on amusement sports activities activities, you may fee rest and entertainment. There are not any right or wrong solutions on this approach, absolutely treasured statistics that will let you higher align your use of time on the facet of your personal values and goals.

However, self-assessment can be a tough manner. It can be hard to face the truth of strategies we spend our time, in particular if we discover that our moves are not aligned with our stated values or desires. This is the time while it's far important to don't forget that self-evaluation isn't a judgment exercising, however alternatively a gaining knowledge of tool. The cause isn't to enjoy horrible about how time has been wasted inside the past, but to gain the statistics you want to make effective modifications inside the future.

Self-assessment additionally can be a effective tool for private responsibility. By maintaining targeted records of the way time is spent, it becomes a first rate deal extra difficult to brush aside or decrease distractions and interruptions. This visibility can offer the incentive to make first rate modifications to how time is controlled.

Self-evaluation is a crucial step in time manage. It affords a clean and unique records of the way time is getting used, well-known conduct patterns, lets in clarify values and priorities, promotes non-public duty, and gives the records had to make powerful and lasting modifications in time manipulate. Without self-evaluation, time manage can end up a guessing challenge, full of assumptions and guesswork. With self-assessment, time manipulate will become a records-pushed device, guided through records and supported thru a deep knowledge of our very very personal man or woman wishes and behaviors.

The reason of the self-evaluation

Self-evaluation is a vital element in powerful time control and turns into the start line for a higher know-how of approaches we use our time. The large reason of the self-assessment is to reveal styles in our each day behavior, which can be stopping us from optimizing the use of our time. In addition, it lets in us to emerge as privy to our cutting-edge time control habits and wherein there are opportunities to decorate.

First of all, self-evaluation facilitates to elevate focus. It presents us with a smooth and practical picture of the manner we're using our time. Without a self-evaluation, we're likely to overestimate or underestimate how plenty time we spend on positive sports activities sports. This misconception can motive inefficient planning and consequently bad time control.

Second, self-evaluation is vital to pattern discovery. By tracking our behavior over the years, we will begin to see styles and tendencies in how we use our time. For example, we might phrase that we will be inclined to be greater inexperienced at effective times of the day, or that positive types of obligations take longer than predicted. These discoveries can be fairly treasured when it comes to making adjustments in our way of coping with time.

In addition, self-assessment allows us to grow to be aware of distractions and challenges. We all face distractions and obstacles that save you us from using our time effectively. However, we aren't constantly aware of what the ones distractions are or how loads time they're costing us. Self-evaluation can help us discover the ones issues and find out solutions to conquer them.

Self-assessment additionally plays a vital feature in placing dreams and monitoring progress inside the route of those goals. Once we recognize how we use our time, we will set more practical dreams and design an action plan to gain them. Additionally, ongoing self-assessment permits us to display screen our development and make modifications as needed.

Finally, self-evaluation allows us observe and broaden. Time control isn't always a skill that is mastered in a unmarried day. It requires exercise, staying strength and, principally, a willingness to study from errors. Self-evaluation gives us the possibility to analyze from our mistakes and to develop as individuals and professionals.

The purpose of the time control self-assessment is to shed moderate on our present day-day behavior and styles, emerge as aware of regions for improvement, set dreams, and show our improvement in the direction of those goals. Through self-assessment, we will learn how to use our time extra efficaciously and successfully, eventually enhancing our productiveness and outstanding of existence.

Steps to make aself appraisal effective

Self-assessment is an important step at the direction to effective time manipulate. This introspection hobby permits you to discover how you're currently the usage of it gradual, what your behavior styles are and what areas of development you can select out. Make aself appraisal Effective time manipulate may be a difficult way, but it is a effective and treasured exercise that could screen beneficial insights and bring about massive development in time manipulate. Here are a few steps you could take to perform aself appraisal powerful.

Identification of modern styles: The first step in aself appraisal powerful is to apprehend how you are using some time in the present. To try this, you could use severa techniques which encompass keeping a every day record of your sports, the usage of time tracking gear, or doing a reflected picture exercise at the prevent of the day. The concept is to seize the reality of the manner a while is shipped most of the distinct duties and duties.

Evaluation of priorities: Next, it's miles crucial to study what your current priorities are and the way those are contemplated for your use of time. Are you spending extra time on obligations which is probably truly important to you? Or do you discover that a while is scattered in activities that do not make a contribution in your long-term desires? This degree of the self-evaluation can require honest and probable uncomfortable mirrored image, however it's miles critical so as to align your use of time at the side of your real priorities.

Recognition of limitations: This step consists of figuring out what factors, whether or not or now not internal or outside, are hindering your capacity to govern a while effectively. Are you coping with constant distractions? Do you find yourself procrastinating on a ordinary basis? Do you experience crushed through using the usage of the workload? By spotting the ones barriers, you could start to broaden techniques to overcome them.

overall performance evaluation: Finding out which duties take you the longest and which of them you whole fast can be a watch fixed-beginning step in self-evaluation. This will will permit you to discover areas in which you could beautify your universal overall performance and others wherein you may have greater room to gradual down and take the time.

Satisfaction assessment: Finally, it is also critical to evaluate your degree of delight collectively together with your present day time manage. Do you revel in constantly harassed and rushed, or as an alternative on top of factors and with a proper balance among paintings and play? Your emotional properly-being is an essential issue to undergo in mind even as dealing with time, for the reason that it is able to have an effect in your productiveness and motivation.

Once you've got completed these steps, you'll have built an extensive picture of your contemporary use of time, the demanding situations thatyou face, regions for development and viable solutions. Armed with this precious statistics, you will be equipped to transport on on your route to higher time manipulate. It is essential to do not forget that self-assessment isn't a one-time exercise, however as an opportunity a normal technique of gaining knowledge of and adjusting.

Chapter 2: Self-Assessment Tools

Time diaries, regularly omitted and underappreciated, are a valuable tool for gaining perception into how we spend our hours, mins, and even seconds within the route of the day. Time diaries act as a replicate that shows our conduct on the subject of time and presents us with an possibility to have a check our workout routines, behavior, and styles.

A time mag is sincerely a report of methods you spend it gradual sooner or later of a given day or week. It's a vital useful resource in time management because it allows you notice precisely in which some time goes. Without correct monitoring, it is easy to expect you are the usage of it gradual effectively, while in fact it may be being fed on with the aid of non-green responsibilities or vain interruptions.

How did the concept of time diaries come approximately? He comes from the arena of employer time manage and personal productiveness. Studies have shown that people regularly have distorted perceptions of tactics loads time they truly spend on splendid sports activities sports. By cautiously recording how they spend their time, they could get a greater realistic and correct photo, after which they could make changes to enhance their efficiency and productiveness.

To get began developing a time magazine, all you need is a pocket ebook or piece of paper and a pen, or perhaps an app for your mobile mobile cellphone or laptop. The aim is to record all of the sports you carry out and the time you decide to every of them.

To some, this may sound tedious and daunting. But recall the advantages. Have you ever come to the give up of a busy day and questioned what you surely completed? Have you had the feeling that time virtually slips away without a few issue good sized having been finished? A time diary let you solve those puzzles.

In addition to providing a easy view of the manner you spend it gradual, time journals also can assist you find out time thieves, the ones sports activities sports that consume quite a few time but do not add any considerable rate. Once you have got got identified those time stealers, you may start taking steps to do away with them or lessen the time you spend on them.

By preserving a time mag, you can advantage precise belief into your conduct and physical activities, permitting you to make knowledgeable selections approximately essential modifications to decorate your efficiency. It is an purpose way of looking at and reading how you use it sluggish and permits you to layout more powerful time management strategies that are appropriate on your life-style.

In the following sections, you can discover ways to use time journals maximum correctly that will help you enhance some time manipulate.

How to use time diaries

A time mag is a powerful device for self-evaluation and knowledge of strategies you use some time. Essentially, it is an in depth report of the sports activities you do during the day, along with how masses time you spend on each one. The intention of the usage of a time diary is to find out your conduct patterns and understand how your hours are dispensed at a few degree inside the day.

Before you begin the usage of a time mag, you want to be clear approximately what you preference to get out of it. Do you need to understand how lots time you spend on effective responsibilities in evaluation to distractions? Are you interested by seeing how an entire lot time is spent on transitions or low charge obligations? Do you want to understand while inside the day you're maximum green? These questions will help you set up the focus of your magazine.

To start a time journal, you need to choose out out a logging tool. You can use some thing from a simple sheet of paper and a pen to a virtual software, relying to your consolation and preference. Remember that the tool you pick out need to be clean to apply and available within the route of the day, thinking about that you can want to make commonplace entries.

An important step is figuring out the duration for which you could preserve the magazine. One day might not be enough to capture your ordinary behavior patterns, so you may also keep in mind journaling for in line with week. During this time, ensure to log all of your sports activities, which includes transitions and breaks. Each get entry to want to encompass the pastime you probably did, the time you started out out and completed, and any notes you need to function.

After you've got were given were given recorded your sports throughout the chosen length, the subsequent step is to investigate the information. Start with the aid of manner of categorizing your sports activities sports into sizeable groups, alongside side paintings, leisure, chores, social media time, and so on. Then upload up the time you spent in each elegance. This will provide you with a clean photo of ways you distribute some time among precise kinds of sports activities.

From there, you could begin to choose out trends and styles. For instance, you is probably aware which you're greater green within the morning, which you're spending extra time on social media than you concept, or that ordinary interruptions are affecting your capacity to awareness on critical duties.

Remember that the motive of a time magazine is not to decide you, however to provide you with the facts you need to make effective modifications on your time management. It's now not about filling each minute of the day with artwork, however about records how your day flows and locating strategies to enhance performance, lessen strain and increase satisfaction.

Finally, as quickly as you have got acquired this statistics, you can use it to make adjustments on your time manipulate. You may also additionally determine to allocate more time to sports which can be vital to you, restriction the ones which is probably distracting or time-ingesting, or attempt awesome productiveness techniques to maximize your excessive-electricity hours. Time diaries aren't a one-period-suits-all solution, but as a substitute a device that you could use frequently to test and regulate some time behavior.

So seize a pen, piece of paper or your favorite app and begin exploring the charming international of your very private weather patterns. You can be surprised at what you could find out and the impact it may have in your life.

Other self-assessment techniques

Self-evaluation is an vital exercise to better recognize how we use our time and the manner we're capable of beautify our manage of it. While time journals are a well-known tool for this venture, there also are distinct self-assessment techniques that may be simply as precious.

Self-assessment thru mission evaluation

One of these techniques is assignment evaluation. This approach entails breaking down your each day sports into character responsibilities and then assessing how lengthy you spend on every of those responsibilities. This allows you pick out obligations which may be taking greater time than they need to be and those in which you may be extra green.

To carry out a assignment assessment, start with the aid of list all the sports activities you do in a ordinary day. Then, for every of those activities, perceive the character duties that make it up. Once you've got this, show how plenty time you spend on each challenge for a few days. This will offer you with an concept of in that you might be losing time or in which you'll be greater green.

Meditation as self-assessment

Another self-assessment tool is meditation. This technique may additionally moreover sound a chunk unusual earlier than the whole thing, however it's far a first-rate manner to advantage more recognition of the manner you operate it slow. By meditating, you are taking a 2nd to disconnect from the outside worldwide and tune in in your inner thoughts and feelings. This helps you to be greater aware about the manner you spend it sluggish and wherein you could make changes for the higher.

To use meditation as a self-evaluation tool, you may begin with only a few minutes an afternoon. During this time, attempt to free your thoughts of distracting thoughts and popularity on the way you spent some time that day. Have you been powerful? Have you committed time to what really topics to you?

Have you felt rushed or forced? By asking the ones questions, you can begin to advantage a higher records of strategies you are handling some time and wherein you can make changes.

Using era for self-assessment

Finally, technology can be a first rate high-quality pal within the self-evaluation of your use of time. There are numerous apps and applications that might song some time automatically, permitting you to look exactly wherein you are spending it sluggish.

Time monitoring apps, like Toggl or RescueTime, can robotically tune the time you spend on one-of-a-type apps and web sites, allowing you to look exactly how you are spending your virtual time. On the opposite hand, productiveness apps like Todoist or Asana allow you to put together your obligations and be aware how a exceptional deal time you spend on particular kinds of paintings.

Additionally, masses of these device offer focused analytics that can show you styles for your time use. For instance, you may discover that you spend most of a while on low-priority responsibilities, or that your productiveness drops at sure instances of the day. By having this records handy, you may make knowledgeable alternatives approximately the way to decorate a while manage.

There are a number of self-evaluation gadget and strategies that you can use to better understand how you use some time. Whether you pick a greater analytical approach, which includes project evaluation, a extra introspective method, which includes meditation, or a technological approach, the secret is to select the technique that works great for you and use it regularly. In this way, you may benefit valuable perception into it sluggish use and take steps to decorate it gradual control.

Chapter 3: Identifying Challenges

How to choose out person worrying situations

The first step in any improvement journey is to actually recognize what wants to be stepped forward. In time manage, this involves identifying your very very personal personal challenges which may be hindering your potential to apply time successfully. By understanding those demanding situations, you could expand particular strategies to overcome them and make greater powerful use of it slow.

The first step in identifying your individual time manage traumatic conditions is self-assessment. It is an intensive examination of methods you operate it gradual on your on a day by day basis. Self-assessment allows you to choose out out styles, conduct, and behaviors that may be contributing to useless time management.

The time magazine is a treasured tool for self-evaluation. You can music the way you spend it slow for the duration of the day, collectively with every artwork and personal sports. With this unique record, you could get a easy picture of the way it gradual is despatched. Look for inclinations and patterns for your each day sports. You can also moreover find which you spend some of time on responsibilities that aren't powerful or do no longer make contributions on your dreams. Or perhaps you discover that there are instances of the day at the identical time as you are a good deal less effective.

In addition to time tracking, it's miles beneficial to reflect on your time manage conduct and behaviors. Do you may be predisposed to procrastinate? Are you without difficulty distracted? Do you feel crushed via the amount of responsibilities you need to carry out? These are all individual worrying conditions that can affect a while control.

Feedback interviews or schooling durations can also be beneficial in identifying time manipulate challenges. Sometimes an out of doors observer can see behaviors or styles which you do not see your self. Ask a colleague, mentor or teach to provide you comments on the way you manage it slow. They is probably able to discover demanding conditions you did no longer understand existed.

Finally, you can use surveys or self-evaluation questionnaires to recognize your character demanding situations. There are numerous on line gadget and quizzes as a way to allow you to decide it slow manage. These device ask you precise questions about your behaviors and behavior, after which offer an analysis of your strengths and regions for improvement.

Identifying your character time control demanding situations is a crucial step towards higher time control. By statistics precisely what limitations are status in your manner, you can begin to expand specific strategies to triumph over the ones worrying conditions and accumulate more powerful time manipulate.

Examples of Common Time Management Challenges

Managing time efficaciously can be a challenge in itself. Here we can describe a series of not unusual boundaries that many humans face whilst trying to manage their time correctly.

procrastination: It is one of the most common traumatic situations. Procrastination can rise up for an entire lot of motives, which includes worry of failure, lack of attention, or in reality a lack of motivation. It's easy to dispose of tasks, in particular ones that appear difficult or overwhelming. This can bring about homework accumulation and might result in strain and anxiety.

Lack of planning: Many humans start their day with out a clear plan or time desk. This can result in dropping time on non-precedence obligations or spending an excessive amount of time on duties that could have required a lot much less time with right making plans.

Multitask: Although it could appear to be multitasking is powerful, the reality is that it regularly consequences in inefficiency. Multitasking can cause errors and decreases the ability to pay interest on a given task.

normal interruptions: These can come from colleagues, emails, cellphone calls, social networks, amongst others. Constant interruptions can interrupt the workflow and purpose wasted time having to go back to the task handy.

Ineffective pressure manipulate: Stress can cause decreased productiveness and the shortage of capacity to govern time efficiently. It is critical to learn how to control stress to save you it from interfering with time control.

Lack of delegation: It isn't unusual for a few human beings to try to do the whole thing themselves. However, this could cause paintings overload and vain time manage. Effective delegation can loose up time for additonal critical responsibilities.

Lack of prioritization: Not all duties are similarly important. Not knowledge how to turn out to be aware of and prioritize critical obligations can reason horrible time manipulate.

Perfectionism: The choice for the entirety to be great can bring about spending too much time on obligations that don't want as a wonderful deal detail. This can prevent well timed very last touch of obligations and duties.

Personal problems:Personal issues, together with health issues or circle of relatives conflicts, can divert hobby from essential obligations and decrease performance in time manage.

Lack of time manage abilties: This consists of now not knowing a way to apply time control gear and techniques, collectively with to-do lists, the Pomodoro Technique, the Eisenhower Matrix, and more.

These are only a few examples of the annoying situations that could upward push up at the equal time as dealing with time. Recognizing and facts these annoying conditions is the first step to overcoming them and improving time control.

Chapter 4: Defining Goals

Setting dreams is a essential part of the manner of efficaciously coping with our time. Goals act as our beacon, directing our moves and permitting us to apply our time extra efficiently and correctly.

Goals offer shape and direction to our lives and sports. They are the compasses that help us navigate the big ocean of time. They provide us a experience of route, retaining us focused on what's vital and stopping us from drifting into sports activities which can be much less green or that do not get us in the course of our goals.

In addition, dreams offer a framework for preference making. When we've were given clean desires, we are capable of without issue decide which obligations are actually well worth our time and energy. This lets in us to prioritize and put together our responsibilities extra correctly, which in flip effects in extra green use of time.

Another essential trouble of putting goals is that they offer us with a deliver of motivation. The tool of strolling toward a aim, in particular one this is big to us, can be especially tough and pleasurable. Every small step we take towards accomplishing our desires can provide us with a feel of achievement and motive, which in turn can inspire us to use our time even greater efficiently.

Setting dreams also can result in more self-recognition. As we reflect on our dreams, we have a look at more about our values, interests, strengths, and weaknesses. This self-know-how is worthwhile, because it permits us to make extra knowledgeable and real choices, every in terms of techniques we use our time and in extremely good additives of our lives.

It is critical to be conscious, but, that placing dreams isn't absolutely about identifying what we need to reap. It moreover includes growing an motion plan and committing to observe it. This issue of cause placing is essential to effective time control, because it lets in us to interrupt our lengthy-term goals into workable short-time period responsibilities, which we can combine into our every day schedule.

Finally, dreams provide us with a technique to diploma our improvement. By defining easy and measurable dreams, we are able to often take a look at how we are progressing in the direction in their fulfillment. This permits us to make adjustments to our interest or goals as crucial, ensuring that our use of time stays powerful and aligned with our lengthy-term desires.

Setting goals is crucial to powerful time manage. Goals supply us route, facilitate decision making, motivate us, foster self-reputation, permit us to growth and follow motion plans, and provide us with a manner to diploma our development. Therefore, if we need to apply our time in the only and green way feasible, we want initially the aid of putting easy and enormous desires.

How to set SMART desires

Defining clean and viable goals is an important element of effective time management. A treasured device for placing goals is the SMART technique, an acronym that stands for Specific, Measurable, Achievable, Relevant, Time-certain. Let's see the manner to use each of those factors to create dreams that assist us manage our time more efficiently.

Specific (Specific): The unique goals are clear and described, which avoids confusion approximately what's predicted to be completed. A specific purpose solutions the questions of what, how, wherein, at the same time as and why. For example, in choice to "I need to be greater powerful," a more precise purpose is probably "I want to finish my project quick each week before the due date."

Measurable: To understand if we've got were given reached a cause, we need a way to diploma our development. A measurable reason consists of quantitative or qualitative standards that assist you to affirm improvement and determine at the same time as the purpose has been carried out. Following the instance above, we can also need to make the motive measurable thru pronouncing, "I need to complete 10 pages of my assignment file every day."

Alcanzable (Achievable): The desires should be practical and viable to accumulate interior our capacities and available resources. If the goal is definitely too bold, we may also moreover experience beaten and emerge as lacking it. On the opportunity hand, if it is too clean, it may not carry any tremendous advantage to our time manipulate. Determining if a cause is capacity also can require an honest evaluation of our capabilities and limitations.

Relevant (Relevant): A applicable goal is one that is aligned with our priorities and lengthy-time period goals. Relevant goals have a clear cause and are in song with other important factors of our lives. The relevance of a cause can be assessed thru asking your self: Will this motive help me drift toward in which I need to move?

Temporarily described (Time-fine): Every motive must have a difficult and fast deadline. This creates a sense of urgency and enables prevent procrastination. Deadlines moreover can help you harm a massive cause into smaller, potential quick-term dreams.

In precis, a SMART purpose for our instance might be: "I want to finish my one hundred-net web page venture record by means of using using November 15, writing 10 pages each day, so I can placed up it every week in advance than the November 22 final date." ".

SMART intention placing is a talent that could take exercise. But once mastered, it will become a effective time manage tool, allowing you to devise, arrange, and prioritize your obligations greater effectively. Let's don't forget that SMART dreams are handiest step one. We additionally need to have techniques and motion plans to gain those desires, which we can have a have a look at in the following chapters of this guide.

Chapter 5: Personalization Of Goals

Identification of your Personal Priorities

On any path to powerful time manipulate, it's far vital to take a step again a good way to mirror and consciousness on what really subjects. Identifying your non-public priorities becomes crucial in this gadget.

To start, we want to apprehend that personal priorities are those factors of our lives that we charge most. They can be as varied as family, fitness, profession, training, relationships, interests, or spirituality, amongst various things. These priorities dictate howwe may also choose spend our time if we had whole freedom to perform that.

Here's a step-through way of manner of-step technique to figuring out your private priorities:

Reflection: Take the time to mirror and don't forget what definitely subjects to you in existence. Ask yourself, what do you fee maximum? What makes you experience finished? What sports activities or roles do you find out a enjoy of purpose in? These questions will help you start to outline your priorities. There are not any proper or wrong answers here; those priorities are private to you.

Assessment: Once you have got had been given meditated in your values and what's important to you, it is time to assess the ones priorities. List all possible priorities that you have identified on your reflected picture. Then, order this list steady with how crucial each object is to you. Here, it's far essential to be honest with yourself. Don't allow certainly one of a type human beings's expectancies have an impact in this assessment.

Time Assignment: After sorting out your priorities, take a 2d to reflect on how your present day use of time aligns with the ones priorities. Are you spending enough time in your top priorities? If the answer isn't any, you could need to reevaluate how you are handling a while.

Goal Setting: Next, use your diagnosed personal priorities to regulate it sluggish manage desires. Every purpose you put must align with as a minimum taken into consideration taken into consideration one among your non-public priorities. This now not great guarantees which you are spending some time in a manner that displays what honestly subjects to you, but it will moreover boom your motivation to benefit the ones goals.

Regular Reassessment: As your lifestyles changes, so will your priorities. It enables to frequently evaluation your priorities and alter your desires and use of time because of this. Consider engaging in a evaluation of your priorities at the least as fast as a yr.

Identifying your personal priorities isn't a manner that can be completed in a single day. It calls for reflected photograph and self-consciousness. However, it is a important issue in developing a time manipulate plan in case you need to now not best assist you be greater effective, however may also will let you steer a lifestyles that displays your proper values and aspirations.

In the give up, it's far approximately constructing a existence that makes you sense fulfilled and content cloth material. When what your priorities are and popularity on them, stress and frustration decrease and also you enjoy extra on top of factors of your life. In addition, carrying out your dreams will become a greater fluid and pleasant manner, because you're running on desires which is probably aligned with what you value maximum.

Goal approach based totally on your strengths and weaknesses

Goal putting is an essential machine in time manage, however for it to be effective, we need to customize it and adapt it to our abilities and boundaries. Our strengths and weaknesses are figuring out factors while defining our goals and the approach to acquire them.

Strengths are the ones capabilities or skills wherein we excel. They are our most powerful weapons, they supply us self notion and performance in certain responsibilities. On the alternative hand, our weaknesses are those areas wherein we've difficulties or limitations. However, with the aid of figuring out them, we're able to paintings on them and flip them into functionality increase opportunities.

To set desires based totally on our strengths and weaknesses, we want to observe the ones steps:

Identification of strengths and weaknesses: The first step is to carry out an sincere and practical self-evaluation. Ask yourself: What am I specific at? What is straightforward for me to do? In what areas do I excel? These are your strengths. Then, recall those regions that you discover hard, the ones responsibilities which you generally tend to do away with or that reason you ache. These are your weaknesses. This self-evaluation manner can be tough, but it's far critical to a customized method to time manipulate.

Setting desires based totally on strengths: Your strengths will provide you with an example of the dreams you can effectively set and gain. For example, when you have strong organizational capabilities, you'll in all likelihood set desires that contain special planning,as Design and observe a time desk of responsibilities. If you are first rate at multitasking, you might set out to address a couple of responsibilities at the equal time.

Construction of development strategies primarily based definitely totally on weaknesses: Instead of ignoring your weaknesses, cognizance on them as opportunities to enhance. If procrastination is a inclined factor, for instance, your cause might be to position into effect strategies that assist triumph over it, collectively with the Pomodoro approach or the two-minute rule. If you discover it hard to live focused, you may set a purpose related to improving this capabilities, probable thru the usage of distraction blocking apps or devoting specific times of the day to duties that require a immoderate stage of attention.

Adjust dreams as you evolve: Time manipulate isn't a static approach, but one which modifications and adapts as you expand and evolve. Over time, your strengths can enlarge similarly, and your weaknesses can grow to be new strengths. Therefore, it is important to often evaluate your goals and regulate them as critical.

Patience and perseverance: Developing talents and overcoming weaknesses do not stand up in a unmarried day. It is a manner that calls for time, attempt and backbone. Don't get discouraged in case you do no longer see immediate outcomes. Patience and perseverance are keys to effective time manipulate.

To conclude, it is vital to remember that no people are the identical, and therefore, no two time manipulate strategies are equal.

What works for one character might not paintings for some special. Goal customization, primarily based absolutely in your strengths and weaknesses, will can help you increase a time management method this is tailored for your unique needs, complements your skills, and allows you to effectively address your weaknesses.

Chapter 6: Customizing Goals Based On Individual Challenges

Analysis of traumatic conditions and the way they've an impact on the definition of desires

Goal setting is a crucial element in time management. However, those dreams are not generated in a vacuum; in fact, they're solid within the crucible of our character demanding situations and existence memories. To make the maximum of our dreams, it's miles essential to understand how our challenges can have an impact on their definition.

First, identifying and analyzing our traumatic situations allows us to define greater relevant and extensive dreams. This is because of the fact our traumatic conditions constitute the areas wherein we want to decorate. For instance, if a routine assignment is a bent to procrastinate, a motive is probably to growth our performance in finishing obligations or to increase conduct that help us keep away from procrastination.

Each project presents an possibility to develop and guide our capabilities. Therefore, in place of perceiving our worrying conditions as insurmountable limitations, we are able to see them as a map indicating regions of our lives that require interest and development. When defining our dreams, the assessment of our demanding situations allows us to transport beyond the big dreams and installation desires which is probably without delay connected to our regions of development.

On the opportunity hand, our annoying conditions also can have an effect on the type of dreams we outline and the way we technique their success. For instance, if one in every of our challenges is stress and anxiety, we can also need to set desires associated with pressure manage, art work-life balance, and looking after our highbrow fitness.

Additionally, analyzing our annoying conditions can also provide us with a greater information of our cutting-edge-day capabilities and limitations. By recognizing our strengths and weaknesses, we're able to set desires which can be regular with our abilities and that, at the identical time, push us to develop and increase. This information also can assist us outline the route to our dreams and pick out out the sources, abilities, and expertise we want to benefit them.

Last but now not least, our disturbing situations ought to have an effect on our commitment and motivation to gain our desires. When we set goals that without delay cope with our challenges, we're more dedicated to undertaking them, as we can see their relevance and importance in our every day lives. Also, as we art work on our demanding situations and word our improvement, this could growth our self-efficacy and self notion in our functionality to manipulate our time successfully.

By reading our challenges and information how they've got an effect on our aim putting, we're able to set greater powerful and applicable desires. These desires, in flip, can assist us enhance our time manage and overcome the demanding situations we're facing. Therefore, in region of averting our stressful conditions, we should face them head on and use them as a guide for our development and growth.

Alignment of goals in conjunction with your way of life and personal values

Aligning desires with way of existence and personal values is a critical factor of effective time control. This way entails ensuring that the dreams you area for yourself are normal on the aspect of your thoughts and the manner you want to live your existence. The alignment of goals with manner of existence and personal values offers motivation, route and which means in your movements, which facilitates more productivity and higher time management.

To get commenced out out, it's far useful to preserve in mind the values and thoughts which is probably maximum crucial to you.

These may be a chain of ethical ideals, which encompass honesty and integrity, or private values which encompass health and circle of relatives. Reflect on what role those values play on your every day lifestyles and the manner they're contemplated on your moves.

The next step is to don't forget your manner of existence. How do you need to spend some time? What activities do you experience and which ones offer you with satisfaction? Perhaps you admire the benefit of an established ordinary, or, conversely, you could do higher with a bendy and dynamic schedule. By taking your lifestyle into attention even as placing your desires, you may strike a stability that allows you to collect your dreams without sacrificing your fine of life.

Once you've got considered your values and lifestyle, you could align them in conjunction with your desires. For instance, in case you price health and wellbeing and experience an energetic way of existence, you may in all likelihood set a goal related to exercising regularly. Or, in case you price persevering with training and feature a hectic life-style, you may set a cause to test one ebook a month.

To align your desires together with your lifestyle and your values, you should additionally take a look at some time availability. How heaps time are you capable and willing to commit to each goal? Can you are making changes on your agenda to house new sports activities? If not, then you can want to reevaluate your wants to better align together with your availability.

It is likewise critical to be bendy and inclined to make changes whilst crucial. As you convert andyou expand up as an individual, so do your values and manner of lifestyles. Therefore, it could be useful to often take a look at your dreams to ensure they hold to align with who you're.

Remember that not all goals want to be massive. In fact, putting smaller, potential desires can be motivating and bring about massive dreams in the end. Even small dreams could have a huge effect at the same time as they are aligned with your values and life-style.

In give up, the alignment of goals in conjunction with your lifestyle and your private values is critical for effective time control. When goals fit in conjunction with your values and manner of lifestyles, you revel in greater stimulated to pursue them and are much more likely to gain them. In addition, it allows you to manual a balanced and amazing life at the same time as strolling closer to your desires.

Chapter 7: Examples Of Time Management Goals

Time control goals for the expert situation

Time management is critical in any art work environment, each to enhance productiveness and to advantage a stability amongst paintings and personal life. The goals associated with time manage within the professional field can variety in keeping with the placement, the volume of obligation and the particularities of the paintings completed. However, there are some general desires that can be tailor-made to almost any expert placing.

Increase productiveness: Productivity can be defined because the functionality to generate notable effects in a given time. A purpose that can be set up in this regard is to increase productivity by manner of a particular percentage internal a specific length. For this, it is crucial to decide the signs and symptoms as a way to be used to degree productiveness.

Lost time cut price: A massive a part of taking walks time is often wasted in non-efficient sports. Identifying and decreasing those sports activities may be a few other profitable goal. For example, you can set a intention to lessen the time spent in unproductive conferences via 50% inner three months.

Efficient control of excessive precedence responsibilities: Prioritizing responsibilities is a important part of time manage. In this experience, the goal of completing all immoderate-priority duties within the running day can be installation, with out the want to increase the day or put off responsibilities for day after today.

Implement and cling to a time manage approach:There are severa time management techniques, together with the Pomodoro approach or the Eisenhower matrix. The desire of approach will rely on the individual inclinations of every expert, similarly to the kind of paintings they do. Once the method is chosen, the intention can be set to take a look at this technique carefully for a high-quality time period to assess its effectiveness.

Improve work-existence stability: This is a important goal to prevent burnout and increase each pastime and private pride. To set dreams in this regard, it is first important to determine what the cutting-edge-day country of labor-life stability is, after which define concretely what modifications you want to achieve.

Remember, for those desires to be powerful they must be SMART: Specific, Measurable, Achievable, Relevant and Temporary. It's now not best important to have dreams, however additionally to ensure the ones dreams are sensible and steady at the side of your art work priorities and wishes. It is likewise crucial to check and alter those goals periodically, thinking about modifications that may get up inside the art work environment. Finally, it is key to keep in mind that achievement in time control isn't always completed in a single day, however requires determination, region and perseverance.

Time manage dreams for the non-public sphere

Goal setting is an vital issue of effective time manipulate in any location of lifestyles, and the personal sphere isn't any exception. Time control goals for the private sphere, like professional goals, should be easy, ability, measurable, relevant and restricted in time, following the SMART criteria. However, the ones desires could be orientated towards improving the exceptional of life, personal satisfaction, the stability between artwork and personal lifestyles, amongst exceptional non-public factors. Let's see some examples.

Improve sleep high-quality:

One of the non-public time manage goals may be to decorate the excellent of sleep. This need to suggest putting in a ordinary sleep time desk, putting apart a relaxing time before mattress, or proscribing display show screen time earlier than bed. These goals can be measured quantitatively, for example, via the massive sort of hours of uninterrupted sleep, or qualitatively, which encompass feeling rested upon waking.

Increase the time dedicated to physical exercising:

Regular exercising is vital to retaining top health and a tremendous mood. A intention is probably to spend as a minimum half-hour an afternoon exercise. This might be measured by means of the use of tracking the time spent in physical activities every week andadjusting it consistent with be critical.

Spend time on interests and enjoyment sports:

In everyday lifestyles, art work and family obligations may want to make it difficult to commit time to pursuits and leisure sports. Therefore, putting unique goals, consisting of spending as a minimum one hour each week on a interest, can help make certain that this time isn't always compromised. This can be done with the aid of assigning a specific time for the interest and respecting it as though it had been an crucial appointment or meeting.

Foster personal relationships:

Another non-public goal is probably to spend greater time on non-public relationships. This may additionally want to mean planning weekly get-togethers with buddies, installing vicinity ordinary date nights along side your partner, or scheduling common calls with own family individuals who live some distance away.

Improve paintings-lifestyles balance:

This is a important intention for optimum people. Effective time manage can assist installation clean boundaries among art work time and private time, thereby decreasing stress and growing lifestyles pleasure.

These are only a few examples of private time control desires. Each person could have unique desires, primarily based on their values, priorities, and private events. The vital issue is that those dreams are clear, sensible and aligned with individual values and priorities. In addition, they need to be trouble to periodic overview and adjustment to mirror any changes in times or private priorities. Effective non-public time control can extensively decorate excellent of existence, non-public delight, and art work-existence balance.

Chapter 8: Planning The Path To Goals

Design a step-with the useful aid of-step motion plan

Developing a step-with the aid of-step movement plan is essential to the powerful awareness of our time control dreams. This technique will assist us genuinely visualize every step we need to take on the path to our dreams, doing away with assumptions and presenting a clean and concrete roadmap.

Definition of theMeta: Before an motion plan can be drawn up, it's far essential to have a smooth vision of the reason to be carried out. This goal have to be SMART, this is, Specific, Measurable, Achievable, Relevant and Temporary. You need to have a easy records of what you are attempting to gain, why it's far critical to you, and what impact it will have to your existence as quickly as it's miles executed.

breakdown ofMeta: Once you have got were given defined your goal, it's time tobreak it down into smaller obligations or steps.These they should be precise actions if you want to frequently bring you in the path of your motive. For instance, if your cause is to lessen procrastination, one step might be to come to be aware of the sports activities that generally reason you to procrastinate.

Task Prioritization: Once you ruin down your aim into smaller responsibilities, you want to prioritize the ones obligations. This may be achieved in masses of approaches, but a not unusual way is to assign each project a diploma of significance and urgency. Those duties which can be every pressing and critical want to be tackled first. The Eisenhower matrix can be a useful tool on this step.

Establishment of Deadlines: After prioritizing your obligations, you need to assign each one a sensible remaining date. These ultimate dates will give you a time body to artwork on and help you avoid procrastination.

Resource Identification: Next, apprehend any assets or tools you can need to finish every mission. This can encompass such things as software software software program, information, help from others, and so on.

Daily movements: After having deliberate your obligations, it's miles vital to perform each day movements that bring you inside the direction of your intention. This should mean setting apart a pleasant amount of time every day to work on your obligations, or growing a every day addiction that lets in you development.

Review and Adjustment: Finally, as you improvement thru your movement plan, you can want to frequently look at your progress and modify your plan if essential. You might also additionally find that excessive fine responsibilities require extra time than you initially idea, or that considered one of a kind responsibilities are not relevant.

Designing a step-via-step motion plan is a mission that requires concept and care. However, by means of taking the time to paintings in this plan, you can significantly growth your opportunities of achieving it slow control goals via means of having a clean and tangible route to observe. This is a worthwhile investment of time, because it will provide you with readability, path, and a sense of reason on your time control journey.

The significance of small achievements at the manner to large dreams

Every super achievement starts offevolved offevolved with a small step. Even the greatest feat, whether or now not it's miles hiking Everest, writing a singular, or building a successful business employer, is finished thru a chain of small cumulative actions that step by step circulate us inside the direction of our final intention. Time manage isn't any exception to this precept.

Small achievements are like bricks that help gather a wall, and every brick is important to the wall's integrity and stability. In the equal way, each small achievement is a important step within the achievement of the larger dreams. The significance of these small achievements lies in numerous elements.

Goal Understanding: Big desires can frequently appear overwhelming. By breaking those goals down into smaller, extra feasible responsibilities, they become goals which might be a lot much less tough to apprehend and cope with. Each small achievement gives us with a clean information of the steps important to attain the bigger motive.

Motivation: Small achievements also are crucial to keep you endorsed along the way. Every success, but small, is proof of development and serves as a stimulus to hold transferring ahead. It is the popularity of every of these achievements that helps us hold self belief and enthusiasm, important elements in any time manipulate method.

Skills and Confidence Development: Each small achievement allows us to exercising and hone the skills vital to gain our massive desires. As we collect small achievements, we no longer most effective enhance our capabilities, but furthermore benefit self warranty in our capabilities. This self assurance is vital to tackling the larger and greater challenging duties that lie ahead at the direction to our dreams.

Time Management and Productivity:Small achievements are fundamental to gaining knowledge of to efficiently control our time. By putting small goals, we are able to plan and control our time extra effectively, which in turn leads us to be more green.

Resilience againstsetbacks: Even with appropriate planning, there will continuously be setbacks. Small achievements can help cushion the impact of these setbacks. When we're going through a setback, we are able to don't forget the small milestones we have got already completed and use them as a reminder that we're able to moving in advance, notwithstanding stressful situations.

Although our massive dreams are what we in the long run want to acquire, it's miles the gathering of small milestones alongside the manner that make that huge success possible. By valuing and acknowledging every small achievement, we no longer excellent get inside the course of our goals, but we furthermore emerge as better stewards of our time, enhance our abilties, growth our self belief, and become greater resilient within the face of setbacks. Therefore, every small success is a victory in itself and an vital thing on the manner to large dreams.

Chapter 9: Progress Tracking Tools

Applications and virtual technology for motive monitoring

In the virtual age we stay in, digital apps and technology have revolutionized the way we tune our desires and our development inside the path of them. These device can be pretty valuable for time manage, as they offer a myriad of competencies designed to assist prepare, plan, and tune obligations and tasks.

Time control and productivity applications: Time management apps like Todoist, Asana, Trello, or Google Tasks offer an green way to prepare your tasks and music your goals. These apps will assist you to create to-do lists, set reminders, and lots of them provide the potential to view your progress through the years. Some advanced apps even let you assign duties to others, which may be very useful in a set environment.

digital calendars: Digital calendars like Google Calendar or Microsoft Outlook are splendid device for scheduling and monitoring some time. You can use them to schedule your duties, set reminders, and be aware at a look how you're spending a while.

Stopwatches and timers: Lots of apps and virtual equipment, like Be Focused, Foresto TomatoTimerThey use the Pomodoro approach. This method consists of strolling for a selected time period (collectively with 25 mins), followed by means of way of way of a brief relaxation. This cycle is repeated severa instances before taking an extended damage. These apps frequently have included timers that you may customize to fit your private desires.

Habit Tracker Apps: These apps, like Habitica or Strides, allow you to set, song, and maintain lengthy-term behavior. Whether you are running on forming a cutting-edge addiction or breaking an antique habit, those apps may be a massive help.

Reflection journals and self-evaluation applications: Apps like Day One orReflectly They will will let you preserve a magazine of your each day sports activities sports, thoughts, and emotions, which can be useful in reflecting for your time manage.

It is crucial to phrase that none of these gear on my own will assure better time management. The key to getting the maximum out of those generation is locating those that paintings remarkable for you, your dreams, and your style of labor. You want to also be conscious that even the best device can't update electricity of will and powerful time manage. These device are there to help you ease the manner, but the real artwork will continuously be as a great deal as you.

Finally, consider that the ones machine ought to moreover be used sparingly. The idea is notoverload you with a massive variety of apps and technologies, however to find out the ones that without a doubt help you track and achieve a while manage goals greater efficaciously.

Traditional development monitoring strategies

In the digital age, it's smooth to overlook conventional development tracking strategies, however in reality, they provide specific blessings and were examined over time. They are technology-unbiased, resultseasily reachable, and offer a tactile and visual way to file and consider development. Although all of us is tremendous and what works for one may not art work for some other, it is crucial to recall those techniques as a possible opportunity on your time control arsenal.

1. The project listing

Task lists are probable the most easy and famous approach of monitoring improvement. This technique includes sincerely writing down the responsibilities you want to finish, allowing you to clearly see what you want to do. When you end a challenge, you can mark it whole, supplying a tangible experience of achievement and development.

2. The time table

Agendas are an extension of mission lists. NoAlone you may hold music of the obligations you want to complete, however you can additionally assign them to unique dates and times. A diary lets in you to devise it sluggish more correctly and ensureyou of which you are making improvement inside the route of your dreams on a day by day basis.

3. The roadmap

Roadmaps are useful for large tasks or long-time period goals. They permit you to smash down a task or aim into smaller, more feasible responsibilities after which chart a course of motion to finish the ones responsibilities. Just like with a planner, you can assign dates to every venture to make certain you are constantly walking in the direction of your purpose.

four. The Progress Journal

Progress journals permit you to tune not most effective your obligations and dreams, however additionally your thoughts and feelings as you discern on them. You can report the limitations you encounter, the answers you find, and the successes you have got. This method may be particularly beneficial for boosting your self-cognizance and getting to know out of your opinions.

five. The graph or table of development

Progress charts or charts offer a visible instance of your development closer to a cause. You can see at a look how lots you've got done and what form of you continue to want to do. This form of monitoring can be specially motivating, as it allows you to tangibly see the development you are making.

These traditional strategies of tracking improvement have many advantages. They are smooth, require no era, and offer a concrete way to look and diploma your progress. It's important to recollect that point manage is a personal know-how and what works tremendous for you can now not paintings as properly for a person else.

Therefore, it is virtually genuinely well worth attempting one-of-a-kind strategies and locating the only that superb fits your dreams and way of life.

Chapter 10: Expectations Vs. Reality In Time Management

Managing frustration on the identical time as expectancies are not met

Start any path of private alternate,as Improving time manage consists of developing expectancies. We choice to acquire powerful results in a positive length. However, reality may not constantly preserve up with those expectancies, and this mismatch can result in frustration. Learning to govern this frustration is essential to staying advocated and persevering with to paintings inside the course of our desires.

Frustration arises whilst there may be a battle among our expectations and fact. In the context of time management, this may arise whilst we assume we will complete a assignment in a single hour, however in fact, it takes three hours. It can also get up whilst we set a time manipulate motive, collectively with working without distractions for an extended term, but locate it to be greater hard than expected.

Understanding the foundation of frustration is step one in managing it efficiently. It is crucial to recognize that our expectations may be primarily based totally on an incorrect or incomplete notion of our abilities, or an insufficient know-how of the mission or purpose handy. Therefore, frustration can be a sign that we need to check and regulate our expectancies to cause them to more sensible and manageable.

To manage frustration, it permits to hold in thoughts that enhancing time manipulate is a device, now not a unmarried event. Change takes time and practice, and it's far everyday to run into bumps along the manner. Instead of viewing the ones limitations as screw ups, we will view them as opportunities to examine and extend. Through these disturbing conditions, we are capable of discover our weaknesses, and boom techniques and competencies to triumph over them.

Also, when encountering frustration, it's miles critical to maintain a nice outlook. We can do that via acknowledging our advances, however small. This can assist preserve our motivation and staying energy.

It is likewise essential to be conscious that effective time manipulate does not mean being first-class. We all have days whilst it costs us moreconcentrate or be inexperienced. Accepting that we are human and that perfection isn't the reason can alleviate frustration.

In this technique, self-care performs a vital function. Relaxation and activity sports can offer a miles-needed respite and help alleviate frustration. Be nice to encompass the ones moments for your every day or weekly ordinary.

Finally, having a aid gadget can be a massive assist. Talking about your frustration with buddies, family, or mentors can offer an out of doors mindset and useful recommendation. In addition, they may be able to provide you the encouragement you want to transport beforehand to your efforts to improve some time control.

Frustration may be a herbal a part of the technique of enhancing time management. However, through understanding its source, preserving a outstanding outlook, looking after ourselves, and searching for resource, we are capable of correctly manipulate frustration and stay on course toward attaining our time control dreams.

Setting expectations primarily based on enjoy and development

The expectancies we set are often a mixture of our desires, desires, assumptions, and once in a while out of doors pressures. In time control, our expectations play a important characteristic in how we plan and use our time. However, it's far vital that we discover ways to regulate our expectations based totally totally on our revel in and development.

At the start, at the same time as we are designing our time manage plans and defining our dreams, our expectations can be very immoderate. This can be powerful because it allows us to be bold and push ourselves to gain extra. But it is able to moreover motive frustration and demotivation if no longer dealt with efficiently. This is wherein enjoy and progress play an crucial position.

Experience is the top notch teacher. As we development on our path to better time control, we advantage experience. We find out how lengthy it without a doubt takes us to finish a challenge, how our sports are interrelated, and what barriers can also furthermore upward push up. This enjoy is valuable because it gives us a sensible picture of tactics we manage our time. We use this enjoy to incredible-tune our expectations and adjust them to what is definitely possible.

On the other hand, our improvement can also help us modify our expectancies. Progress is not normally linear. There can be days whilst we acquire extra than predicted and others even as we do no longer acquire the whole thing we got right down to do. It is essential not to be discouraged through the usage of the a good deal less green days. Instead, we must view them as learning opportunities.

Regular tracking of our development permits us apprehend our fluctuations in productivity. We may additionally moreover discover that we're extra powerful at excessive first-class instances of the day, or that positive obligations take longer than anticipated. By statistics those versions, we are able to realistically regulate our expectations.

Adjusting our expectancies primarily based on enjoy and development moreover approach acknowledging our enhancements. When we see that we are engaging in greater in tons less time, or that we're coping with to balance our sports activities more successfully, we need to alter our expectations upwards. This will assist us maintain moving ahead and encourage us to keep improving our time manipulate.

Setting expectations need to not be visible as a failure or a step backwards. Rather, it is an crucial part of effective time management. As we advantage more enjoy and information approximately how we paintings and the way we manipulate our time, our expectancies grow to be more correct and useful. Instead of being a deliver of frustration, they grow to be a device that permits us plan and use our time in the simplest way viable.

Finally, it is important to endure in thoughts that everybody is particular. What works for one may not paintings for some other. Therefore, our expectancies ought to be based totally mostly on our personal enjoy and improvement, and now not on comparisons with others. By doing so, we are capable of be respecting our very very own abilties and barriers, and we can be in a higher position to govern our time effectively.

Chapter 11: Time Management And Productivity

Effect of Good Time Management on Productivity

Productivity is not pretty a high-quality deal doing more in an awful lot much less time. At a essential degree, productiveness is set engaging in more of what topics. This is wherein correct time management shines as a crucial element to enhance productivity in all regions of our lives, every non-public and expert.

Time is a finite useful aid. Regardless of ways diligent we are, every person have the equal 24 hours in an afternoon. However, how we use the ones hours determines our diploma of productivity. Effective time control lets in us to make best use of this finite aid, which in flip improves our productivity.

There are numerous key elements in which accurate time control may additionally moreover have a proper away and high-quality effect on productivity.

Task Prioritization: Good time control consists of classifying our responsibilities based totally on their significance and urgency, allowing us to recognition on what honestly subjects. This prioritization gadget reduces the opportunity of losing time on sports that do not make a contribution to our desires. As a result, we are greater effective, for the cause that our energies are channeled inside the path of the responsibilities that convey us closer to our goals.

discount ofStress: Work overload and tight last dates may be enormous belongings of strain. However, powerful time control can help control this pressure through presenting a form that makes it easy to emerge as privy to duties that want to be finished and the time required to accomplish that. This creates a experience of control, which reduces strain and, in turn, will increase productivity.

Increase in Work Quality: With effective time management, we aren't pressured to rush our paintings to meet final dates. This lets in us to spend good enough time on each mission, resulting in higher quality work. When the satisfactory of work is excessive, we are more green due to the reality the need for revisions or corrections is decreased.

Space for Creativity: Efficient use of time additionally opens area for reflected picture and creativity, which may be vital for innovation and trouble fixing. When we are not rushed or overwhelmed through way of to-dos, our minds are unfastened to discover new ideas, that may purpose more creative and inexperienced answers.

Improvement of the Balance among Work and Personal Life: Productivity isn't limited to artwork or check; it is also applicable to our private lives. Effective time manipulate can help us higher stability our artwork and private duties, permitting us time to loosen up, recharge, and experience the sports activities we love. This balance can boom our hooked up happiness and pleasure, which in flip can boom our productiveness in all regions of life.

Improved Decision Making: With a easy vision of our priorities and the time wished for each assignment, we are able to make more knowledgeable picks approximately the manner to allocate our time. This can result in an boom within the efficiency with which we perform our obligations, improving common productivity.

It is critical to be aware that proper time control does now not absolutely mean being busy all of the time. It's approximately beingstrategics in how we use our time, ensuring that we are spending this valuable useful useful resource on duties that carry us in the direction of our desires and values. With specific time manipulate, we are able to increase our productiveness, now not simply with the resource of doing more, but with the resource of using doing what surely subjects.

Chapter 12: Common Myths About Time Management

Debunking common myths about time control

Time control is a topic that has been studied for years and, as such, has spawned a number of myths and misunderstandings. In order to control our time efficiently, it's far crucial to confront and debunk these myths.

Myth 1: Being busy is much like being efficient.

Being busy does no longer usually equate to being green. The delusion that constant motion and perpetual interest are symptoms and symptoms and signs and symptoms and signs of productiveness can purpose inefficient use of time. In truth, being too busy can reason fatigue and burnout, which decreases productiveness. Productivity is finished with the aid of going for walks smarter, now not extra tough. This manner that specialize within the wonderful-precedence responsibilities that without a doubt circulate the needle in the direction of our dreams, in place of absolutely filling our time with art work.

Myth 2: Multitasking is inexperienced

Many maintain in thoughts that multitasking is an effective manner to deal with more than one duties at the identical time. However, studies display that multitasking can actually reduce productivity by way of using using as much as forty%. When we strive to multitask, our brain is compelled to continuously switch its consciousness from one challenge to any other, which could drain our highbrow power and decrease performance. Instead, it is greater effective to recognition on a unmarried assignment to finishing touch in advance than shifting directly to the subsequent.

Myth three: Everything is urgent

Poor time control regularly stems from the misconception that the entirety is an emergency and desires to be dealt with proper away. In fact, few obligations require on the spot hobby. Treating everything as an emergency can result in fatigue, strain, and decreased brilliant of hard work. Rather than fall into the "false urgency" trap, it's far essential to examine to distinguish among in reality urgent obligations and people that can be scheduled for later.

Myth four: There isn't always sufficient time

Many human beings take into account that they really do now not have sufficient time to do the whole thing they need or need to do. However, this is often a problem of belief in preference to reason fact. We all have the identical 24 hours in a day, however how we select out to apply that aspect can range drastically. Often the sensation of "not having sufficient time" comes from a lack of prioritization and time management, now not the amount of time itself.

Myth five: Time control is innate

Some may think that the potential to govern time successfully is an innate potential that some people certainly personal, at the equal time as others do not. That's now not actual. Time manipulate is a knowledge that can be located and advanced with workout and patience. No rely how you have got got controlled some time inside the past, you could usually discover ways to do better.

Debunking those myths can open up a modern route to approach time manage in a extra sensible and wholesome manner. By releasing ourselves from the ones improper ideals, we permit ourselves the possibility of locating and adopting time manage strategies that in reality artwork for us. Not all strategies will art work for every person, so it's important to find out which strategies paintings wonderful so that it will your private and professional lifestyles.

How myths can restriction your powerful time management

Myths, on many events, can be visible as truths rooted in society and are frequently volatile to our effective manage of time.

Although a few may also additionally have a degree of truth, often those myths have a propensity to misinterpret truth and restriction our capacity to govern our time efficaciously.

We will begin with one of the maximum common myths: "Multitasking is inexperienced". Although in principle it is able to appear that multitasking is an excellent use of time, the reality is that our attention is cut up amongst one-of-a-kind sports, reducing the overall performance in they all. When seeking to tackle multiple responsibilities concurrently, we're prone to making mistakes, which ends up in wasted time having to correct them. This fantasy, therefore, can avoid our powerful time manipulate by way of the usage of manner of making us agree with that we're being inexperienced, while in fact we are being a whole lot a good deal less efficient.

Another fantasy that would push back our time control is: "There is constantly time to do it later." This myth motives us to procrastinate, which often effects in procrastination. This dependancy can result in pressure and anxiety, for the cause that responsibilities collect and we have to complete all of them on the give up, generally in a limited time. By believing this delusion, we lose the opportunity to govern our time efficiently and riskoverload us of hard paintings.

A zero.33 myth really worth citing is: "Time is coins." This myth can lead us to accept as true with that we need to continuously be busy to be powerful, that would bring about the denial of enjoyment time and relaxation. Rest time is crucial for our intellectual and physical health, andskip it is able to result in burnout and reduced productiveness in the end. Therefore, believing this delusion can be adverse to our functionality to control time efficiently.

It is critical to preserve in thoughts that each person has a totally specific manner of managing their time and what works for one may not art work for some unique. A fable may also look like a ultra-modern reality, however in fact, it is a generalization that does not keep in mind the distinctiveness and area of facts of all people. By debunking the ones myths, we supply ourselves the opportunity to discover and adopt time manipulate techniques that higher align with our specific desires and situations.

Myths can be barriers in our time control, restriction us and every so often lead us inside the incorrect path. However, thru spotting them as such, we're able to triumph over them and boom effective time control techniques that in shape our person desires. It is crucial to significantly query and evaluate those entrenched beliefs to save you them from hindering our capability to control time efficaciously.

Chapter 13: Importance Of Flexibility In Time Management

How to increase a bendy mind-set in time control

Flexibility is a important expertise in time management. It allows human beings to conform to sudden conditions, switch duties efficiently, and stay resilient to disruptions. Developing a bendy time control thoughts-set isn't any easy mission, however with the proper techniques and strategies, it's miles possible to domesticate this capability to decorate productiveness and artwork-lifestyles stability.

First of all, it's miles important to recognize that flexibility in time manipulate does now not suggest lack of form or planning. On the alternative, it's miles about building a plan that has room for modifications and adjustments. It is accepting that the surprising takes place and being prepared to address it without greatly affecting your popular goals.

To growth a bendy mind-set, one of the first steps is analyzing to govern and take transport of exchange. Change is a regular in lifestyles, and getting to know to simply accept it and adapt to it's miles critical. It may be beneficial to workout adaptability in low pressure situations so you are higher prepared while extra difficult conditions stand up.

In this sense, self-information is essential. Knowing your very very very own talents and limitations will can help you tailor your plans and dreams greater correctly. You can, as an instance, understand that it takes you longer than anticipated to finish sure duties, or that you are more effective at advantageous times of the day. Take advantage of this self-expertise to adapt your plans and schedules.

In addition, flexibility moreover implies being capable of re-examine and regulate your desires and priorities. Sometimes converting situations can make certain dreams a whole lot less essential or maybe beside the point.

Being capable of recognize this and regulate your goals and priorities because of that is a critical a part of bendy time control.

Practicing staying power and calm also can help boom flexibility. Unforeseen occasions can bring about pressure and frustration, which in turn need to make it difficult to conform to new times. Practicing stress control strategies, in conjunction with meditation or everyday workout, can help maintain you calm in some unspecified time in the future of times of change and uncertainty.

Finally, at the same time as time manipulate is regularly focused on productivity, flexibility moreover approach knowing while to take a break. Sometimes the most effective opportunity can be to take a smash or perhaps delay a task for all all over again. Learning to understand these moments and allowing your self to rest or switch obligations can be very beneficial for your commonplace properly-being and lengthy-time period effectiveness.

Developing a bendy time control thoughts-set is an ongoing method, one that calls for exercising and electricity of will. But with the resource of incorporating the ones strategies and techniques into your every day existence, you could beautify your ability to control exchange,adapt to new sports and in the end manipulate some time more successfully.

Examples of ways flexibility can enhance time manage

People often are looking for to paste to rigid schedules or properly specific to-do lists which will beautify their productiveness. However, the modern global is specially dynamic and complete of unforeseen activities, which means unplanned duties and interruptions are inevitable. The key to effective time control isn't to dispose of those contingencies, but to expand the capability to evolve to them. Below are numerous examples of ways flexibility can enhance time manage.

Adaptation to surprising changes: Imagine you have got a meeting scheduled for the forestall of your workday, however it receives canceled on the final minute. Instead of having annoyed, a flexible technique might will let you use that factor to artwork on certainly one of a type duties that want hobby. The sudden alternate to your time desk does not come to be a barrier on your productiveness, but an possibility to growth in specific duties.

Taking benefit of moments of idea: Suppose you are running on a present day assignment and a wave of concept hits you at an unscheduled time. If you have got were given got the ability toreset your agenda, you could take advantage of that height of creativity to supply your great paintings, in preference to equipped until your "allocated time" for progressive art work.

Stress mitigation in excessive stress conditions: High-pressure conditions are commonplace in lots of labor environments. If an emergency arises and also you need to divert your hobby from your deliberate responsibilities, flexibility will allow you torearrange your day with out which include useless strain. For instance, if you are a health practitioner and an emergency arises on the clinic, a flexible method have to permit you to rearrange your unique obligations with out feeling overwhelmed.

Promoting a better art work-life stability: A flexible method to time manage assist you to higher integrate your paintings and private responsibilities. For example, in case your toddler has a faculty performance within the center of a weekday, the ability can also want to assist you to work from home or rearrange some time desk to attend the overall performance and then make up paintings time at over again.

Optimization of private power performance:People have particular work prices and power degrees all through the day. Some are more powerful within the morning, while others artwork higher in the afternoon or at night time. If you have the flexibility to arrange your time desk in line with your personal natural rhythms, you may use your moments of higher strength for responsibilities that require more reputation and try, because of this enhancing your productivity.

These examples show how a bendy method to time manipulate can beautify productiveness, lessen stress, and facilitate a better artwork-existence balance. But it's miles critical to remember that flexibility does not suggest loss of shape. It's approximately having a form that can be adjusted and tailor-made as desired, so that you can reply effectively to the surprising and take gain of opportunities as they rise up.

Chapter 14: Dealing With Interruptions And Distractions

Techniques to reduce and control interruptions

Interruptions are an inevitable part of lifestyles, each in my view and professionally. Despite this, there are powerful strategies to restriction and manipulate the ones interruptions, allowing you to hold a everyday approach and improve a while management.

Interruption Identification

The first aspect you should do to deal with interruptions is to become aware of which can be the maximum commonplace and disruptive. For example, they'll be mobile phone calls, emails, mobile notifications, surprising visits, amongst others. Identifying those interruptions will allow you to extend techniques to govern them correctly.

Establishment of Schedules for Communications

An effective method is to set up unique hours to manipulate effective communications. For instance, you could allocate a block of time for your every day time table to check and reply to emails or messages. This limits the sort of times those responsibilities interrupt your day and lets in you to hobby for your most critical responsibilities outside of these hours.

Use of Technology in Your Favor

Technology can be a primary deliver of interruptions, however it could moreover be your satisfactory friend in minimizing them. Many devices and apps have "do now not disturb" or "silent mode" settings that may be used all through intervals even as you need to hobby on a assignment. There also are apps designed that will help you restriction digital distractions through blocking get proper of entry to to outstanding apps or web sites for a hard and rapid time body.

Creation of a Suitable Work Environment

The physical surroundings in that you art work may want to have a huge impact on the huge type of interruptions you face. Consider using noise-canceling headphones in case you're in a noisy environment, or installation a quiet, distraction-free place of job if possible. Put up a sign or alert human beings round you in case you are inside the center of an critical mission and want to avoid interruptions.

Outage Management Training

Finally, not all interruptions can be averted. For those situations, it's far beneficial to have a direction of motion. Learning to mention "no" lightly however firmly, or to barter a more reachable time, can be surprisingly beneficial. Interruption management can also encompass the capacity to short pass back to the project you were doing after being interrupted. The reason is to restriction the effect an interruption has for your attention and productiveness.

Through outage identification, proactive planning, inexperienced use of technology, and development of control competencies, you can limit the wide variety and impact of outages for your each day. This will not best allow you to boom your productiveness, but furthermore enhance your properly-being thru decreasing the stress and frustration related to the normal interruption of your duties.

How to turn distractions into effective breaks

One of the precept issues whilst managing time is coping with distractions. Some research have tested that distractions can devour as heaps as 50% of our powerful time. However, this doesn't suggest that every one distractions are inherently terrible. Some distractions may be a deliver of relaxation, creativity and motivation, so long as they'll be handled properly.

The first step in turning distractions into inexperienced breaks is to recognize that now not all distractions are created identical. There are one in every of a type varieties of distractions, and their effect can range depending on the context in which they stand up.

Distractions can be out of doors or internal. External distractions can encompass interruptions from coworkers, cellular notifications, or history noise. Internal distractions, however, come from our very private thoughts and impulses, like the temptation to test social media or worry approximately a to-do.

Once we recognize the form of distraction we are coping with, we are capable of make greater knowledgeable choices about a way to control it. For instance, we may also moreover decide to address outside distractions via converting our artwork surroundings or via setting up clear policies approximately interruptions. In the case of inner distractions, we're capable of resort to strategies along with meditation or mindfulness to beautify our capability to pay attention.

Next, we should recollect whether or not or no longer the distraction may be a supply of relaxation or restoration. Productive breaks are people who assist us regain our electricity and cognizance. These breaks can include sports sports like taking a stroll, listening to track, getting a few workout, or perhaps playing a mobile recreation.

To turn a distraction proper right into a powerful damage, we need to set easy limitations. This way figuring out earlier how a extremely good deal time we are able to spend at the relaxation hobby and ensuring that it does now not come to be an evasion of our obligations. We should moreover choose out rest sports that without a doubt help us to recharge our power and not without a doubt to put off our duties.

Finally, we can make our effective breaks even greater beneficial by using incorporating activities that help us gain our prolonged-term desires. This can encompass studying a ebook related to our concern of hard work, operating towards a talent we want to expand, or possibly meditating to enhance our interest and emotional properly-being.

In stop, distractions aren't constantly awful. If we understand and control them correctly, we are able to turn them into powerful breaks that help us decorate our efficiency and satisfaction at art work. However, the essential thing to achieving this is to hold a stability, ensuring that our breaks do not take us a ways from our responsibilities or prevent us from accomplishing our goals.

Chapter 15: Is Time Getting Out Of Hand?

We be aware of the most excessive times on information programs with amazement; those are tales of folks that get so enraged approximately an reputedly little occurrence that they attack and harm or perhaps homicide each other character because of their wrath. One of the most common factors of this condition is what's referred to as "street rage," however there are numerous exceptional manifestations, and they'll encompass almost any human interest. All that is essential is at the least people, a spark, and a participant who takes the whole lot an entire lot too appreciably that allows you to start a fire. In addition, it might seem that those components can be received and are delivered into contact with every different at an all at once immoderate rate.

These are extreme examples of what is regularly called "hurry infection," this is an traumatic temper delivered on thru the perception that there isn't always enough time in the day to do all that needs to be completed. Some humans are so centered on reaching their targets that even the maximum common and common form of setback can also moreover additionally throw them proper right into a murderous frenzy that leaves them without the capacity to suppose absolutely. We are comforted by way of way of the understanding that we are more affordable, more balanced, and similarly adjusted than these top notch human beings, and we find ourselves wondering how the ones one of a kind human beings can lose manipulate so fast and in reality. We do no longer permit even the smallest disruptions throw us off, and we exercising general command over each our emotions and our conduct.

Are we, in all honesty? Even if the bulk people, to our brilliant remedy, aren't prepared to dedicate mayhem at the same time as topics do no longer pass our manner, a superb shape of us have a excellent hassle managing occurrences that knock us off route and interfere with our desires. The United

States of America is a country of overachievers whose lives are continuously done in speedy ahead. As a end result of getting little time for making plans, masses humans have end up professionals in coping with crises, as we have been dashing to region out hearth after hearth. Every one folks is reliant on in a single day delivery and speaking via the use of email, fax, and the mobile phone. We are typically connected manner to personal virtual assistants and BlackBerries, and we time our duties proper right down to the minute if you need to cram them into our already packed agendas.

To show, in this unique location, you have to use all of your available going for walks power surely to preserve your present day-day position. You are going to have to run at least times as fast as that in case you want to head somewhere else.

Through the Looking Glass

This is a brief and smooth test to determine whether or not or now not or not you're stricken by moved short illness. To calculate how prolonged it takes for one minute to bypass, all you want is a timekeeper to maintain tune of the clock on the equal time as you are making your exceptional bet. Please sit down down and make your self at domestic. It does not be counted if you take a look at your watch or begin counting "one Mississippi, Mississippi." . . Your companion will let you know to "Go" to begin the check, and even as you be given as real with that one minute has lengthy beyond, you may exclaim "time's up!" "

Feel free to provide it a bypass.

How an prolonged way did you get? Have you been underestimating the time period which you had been geared up? If it truely is the case, you'll be a part of the bulk. During carefully placed trying out, the vast majority of contributors shouted "time's up! " after a quick pause of spherical fifteen seconds. At the very least one of the subjects believed that the minute had already surpassed after sincerely seven seconds. Only some of people managed to very last the entire minute.

If we have been as terrible at predicting the amount of vicinity available to us as we seem like at estimating the quantity of time, we might constantly run into one another.

Another take a look at is furnished below. Your partner will time you at the identical time as you stay however for one minute and sixty seconds with out mission any interest. In your opinion, how extended does that minute of compulsory idleness appear to be? Do you discover that even simply one minute of silence makes you uncomfortable?

It now looks like an eternity every time a minute passes. Nanoseconds, or one billionth of a second, are the gadgets which can be presently used to diploma time. "Teraflops," regularly known as trillions of computations ordinary with 2nd, are the operations that may be executed with the aid of the usage of manner of supercomputers.

One more examination. It takes a piece longer than the best-minute exercise to finish, but it isn't tough, and you do now not need a associate to carry out it. Tomorrow, as you cross about your day, you could get via without wearing an eye fixed fixed if you just leave it at domestic. Take a while to recollect these questions about the stop of the day.

1.When you did no longer want or want to recognize the time, did you find yourself checking your wrist even in case you knew it already?

2.Even despite the fact that you have been no longer carrying a watch consistent, did you find it tough to preserve track of the time?

You are all over again within the majority of human beings in case you responded "positive" to the number one question however "no" to the second one question. The majority human beings have come to be used to monitoring the passage of time in more and more minute increments as we rush ourselves from one pastime to every unique, assembly one reduce-off date after each different and scheduling one appointment after every other. Even the interesting sports are planned in advance. Because this non-stop monitoring has advanced proper right into a addiction for us, we're definitely ignorant of how time-pushed we've were given end up.

In current society, the undertaking consists of now not being aware about the cutting-edge-day second. There are everyday reminders gift. There are clocks searching down at us from the walls of the administrative center, and watches are bobbing on the wrists of just about truly all people we are available in contact with. The man or woman analyzing the time on the radio does it in a repetitive manner, despite the fact that with a few moderate variances. "It is seven 16, 16 mins after the hour of 7 o'clock, forty-4 mins earlier than 8." This is what our pc systems show while the time is entered.

Show us the time while we take a look at in, and preserve us knowledgeable of the exact quantity of time that has exceeded even as we are working. While we're using to our next appointment, neon lights flash the time and the present day-day temperature at us.

Take a hint harm from what you are doing and consider this fact: in the beyond, there had been neither watches nor clocks. People from all over the hamlet in England rushed to the town rectangular to look the notable sight of the primary public clock being established there. And it truly had a unmarried appendage! You had been first-rate able to telling time to the closest hour.

Is it truely possible for us to conceive of a worldwide without timekeepers? Almost absolutely now not. We aren't pleasant privy to the passage of time; alternatively, we're pressured through time, besotted via time, and ate up in time.

Getting a rush from the adrenaline

Another honest evaluation to help stumble upon a suspected case of moved speedy contamination is verified right here. Simply imply whether or not or no longer you compromise or disagree with the following announcement: "I perform better beneath pressure."

It appears that almost all oldsters have this view. We spotlight the awesome on our resumes, coupled with "very brought about self-starter," and we boast about our capacity to art work nicely even though faced with pretty stringent time constraints.

Some parents select out out up this dependancy in college, ready to write down that time period paper until the day earlier than it is due, pulling an all-nighter, and going to beauty bleary eyed, bedraggled, but smugly self-satisfied that some other project has been successfully met. This is a dependancy that a number of us pick out up in university. Because we are simply aware of our very personal brilliance, we comply with this mind-set to different elements of our lifestyles, moving on with self-warranty and the expectation that others might probable subsequently widely recognized the fee of our competencies.

You, too? After you have accumulated your self, you should check thru that paintings all over again. Your high-quality? When you rush through a undertaking, the fantastic of the artwork which you do decreases, and also you need to be sincere with yourself and understand it.

You are also experiencing pain. You be troubled through a shape of movement infection that isn't always the sort that makes you experience queasy in reaction to the rolling of a deliver, but alternatively a dependency on movement and speed that could become nearly as effective as a right dependancy. This shape of movement infection manifests itself in each your body and your thoughts.

The word "time for amusement" has advanced into an oxymoron. We have one very prolonged workday, that is damaged up with the resource of the usage of moved rapid food and careworn nights of sleep but does now not in any other case offer any treatment. The excellent people who seem to have time to laze about are the fashions inside the garb catalogs.

We Americans take shorter and less vacations, and we function our paintings with us, manner to our beepers and cell telephones, in addition to our fax machines and e mail. However, notwithstanding the fact that our home laptop systems are extensions of the place of work, the truth that we are capable of work at home suggests that we're constantly running.

We rush through lifestyles and try to skip "amusing" topics off the to-do list as fast as viable, so entertainment now not has the identical due to this as it as soon as did. Even our leisure sports sports, which includes bodily education, forced "rest," and competitive pastimes (who plays golfing with out keeping rating?), have taken on a more critical and realistic tone. Even viewing birds has evolved right proper into a aggressive sport in current years.

Simple symptoms and horrifying outcomes of hurry contamination

Where do you stand? Have you come back go into reverse with a case of the jitterbugs? Among the signs and symptoms are:

anxiety

depression

fatigue

appetite swings

repetitive behaviors and thoughts (repetitive movements which can be hard or perhaps no longer feasible to stop)

a lack of motivation to take a break, in positive times even an incapacity to attain this the lack of potential to relaxation even after one has completed their gadget for the day

This isn't a pleasant aspect, however it will now not result in loss of existence. Don't permit skip. It receives worse. We are all required to run the strange dash, make the immovable closing date, and address the sudden emergency on occasion. And we're capable of do it with out inflicting any lengthy-time period damage or inefficiency. It is even viable for it to be exciting.

But maintain to pressure in that fast lane until it will become a addiction, at which trouble you run the chance of the subsequent:

excessive blood strain

illnesses of the coronary coronary heart

migraines

insomnia

digestive troubles

stroke

The tension that comes from in search of to keep up with existence's fast pace compromises the immune device by interfering with the frame's regular production of T lymphocytes (white blood cells). This effects in an improved chance of growing infections and cancers.

Living within the fast lane has the potential to make one unwell. It is even able to killing you.

Reports Of The "Death Of Work" Premature

Arthur Schlesinger, Jr., a nicely-reputable historian and social commentator, posted an essay in The Saturday Evening Post in 1959 in which he advised Americans of "the onrush of a modern-day-day generation of enjoyment." Were you warned? In 1967, outstanding sociologists testified in the the front of a U.S. The Senate's Labor Subcommittee end up asked to forecast with a excessive degree of reality that the average American employee may want to fast be able to take benefit of a twenty--hour artwork week or a twenty--week art work 3 hundred and sixty five days.

These specialists anticipated that a giant range dad and mom may be retiring by way of using the age of 38, and the primary impediment we'd face, as Schlesinger had expected 8 years earlier, will be the way to efficiently control all of our spare time.

These forecasts convey to thoughts the selection made through an government at Decca Records to bypass up the possibility to signal a storage rock band from England for the reason that "guitar music is on the verge of extinction."

The band's call have become The Beatles, and they were a success but clearly having three guitars and a drum set. The authorities from Decca have come to be the most effective one leaving the building at that factor.

How is it that such a variety of so-known as professionals were given it so wrong? What got here to skip? Why wasn't the Age of Leisure ushered in through manner of our amazing technology as an alternative?

We made off with the cash. Instead of taking a few day without work, we determined to hobby on enhancing our material level of existence.

You do not keep in thoughts making that particular selection, do you? It's feasible that you had been in no way presented with the opportunity, at least not in the ones words. But in preferred, the majority parents decided on to artwork longer as opposed to shorter hours, and in addition people went to artwork. As a result, in place of ushering in an Age of Leisure, we ushered in an Age of Anxiety and hooked up the standard of the 2-earnings domestic.

Particularly girls were stricken by the limited quantity of time available. You had been expected if you need to have a flourishing circle of relatives further to a a achievement device. However, this did no longer end up the case. However, while those superwomen were given domestic following a long day on the workplace, they had been met with the beneficial resource of a mountain of chores that needed to be completed. They ended up operating 24 hours an afternoon, seven days in step with week, it is equal to a double shift. And girls who raised their kids on my own in no way had a choice. If they did not do it, it failed to get completed.

There was a top notch deal of stress on us to pick out out the coins, regardless of whether or now not or now not or now not we made the choice of our very very own will. And it paid off; as our salaries stepped forward, so did our diploma of life, and nowadays each home is stuffed to the brim with diverse home equipment, technological devices, and different things. . . Stuff. We choice pretty much the whole lot that is modern-day day, and we throw away the entirety this is broken, worn, or virtually out of style with such regularity that our landfills are overflowing with waste merchandise.

People that located forth masses of effort are rewarded with positions that they could stay, on the facet of social approbation and more money. When our supervisor tells us to "art work smarter, no longer more tough," what she truely way is "get more finished," and that lets in you to collect that, we ought to installed greater attempt similarly to walking smarter. When we have been requested to take over the task of a colleague who had certainly left the corporation (possibly due to "downsizing" or possibly "rightsizing"), we have been given the subsequent advice: "You can accomplish greater with an lousy lot less." But it's far a lie. You can not do greater with a bargain plenty less assets. You can high-quality do more work if you have extra time, strive, and electricity to dedicate to it; however, that beyond regular time, attempt, and power has to go back from somewhere, and it has to come back returned from different factors of your existence, together with conversation, sleep, and play.

We Have Seen the Enemy, and It Is Us

Is it all of the fault of the managers? To be honest, no. The haste contamination is a few component that we've were given, to a big quantity, added upon ourselves.

We determine our private importance and the charge we offer to the area primarily based mostly on how busy we're. The devices on our to-do list provide the framework internal which we make revel in of our revel in of reason and the which means of our lives. We have famous the unambiguous societal message that folks who are busy are profitable humans, and possibly even morally higher human beings. "Idle palms are the satan's workshop," because of the reality the vintage pronouncing is going.

It isn't actually peer strain. Deep down inside us, quiet makes us demanding. Although we might in no way say it, a superb hundreds oldsters virtually dread our time off and look in advance, in private, to the begin of the workweek on Monday. Because we worry the capability risks of unscheduled entertainment, we make sure that every and each hour is productively spent.

We despise the idea of "losing time" and like to talk approximately "saving time" and "spending wonderful time" instead. This is due to the fact we act as although time have been coins, or no much less than a commodity just like cash, which has the capability to be each stored up or frittered away.

"Half of our lives are spent seeking to fill the time that we have squandered through speeding thru lifestyles searching out methods to rescue it," this proverb says.

Will Rogers turned into an American stand-up comedian and philosopher who lived from 1879 to 1935.

Where exactly have you "saved" all of this "time," despite the fact that? It is invisible to you. It isn't viable to comprehend it together with your fingers. You cannot simply located it in a field and bury it someplace out of sight for protection.

What is time, exactly?

Here is a short and easy approach to determine what time it is in your location. Make a phrase of a few fantastic expressions which have the word "time" in them. Make them illustrative of the manner you word the passage of time on your life. To provide actually one example, you may write:

You also can say something like, "I'm trying to discover ways to use my time wisely," or

"I've observed that I can keep time with the useful useful resource of writing a to-do list each morning earlier than I go to paintings," or "I've determined that I can keep time with the aid of way of..."

"After supper is once I most customarily discover myself wasting time."

You want to go in advance and jot down a few in the time you've got. (I assure that the

125

bodily activities on this ebook are presupposed to educate you a few aspect beneficial about your relationship with time, that is the number one interest of this e-book.)

Now rephrase each of the previous sentences, but this time update all occurrences of the word "time" with the phrase "existence." See what you give you.

In our cases above, we would get:

☐ "I'm searching for to discover ways to spend my existence as it should be."

☐ "I've determined that I can keep life by way of growing a to-do listing."

☐ "I normally have a tendency to waste lifestyles after dinner."

The element to this little parlor trick? (Did you suspect of it as a "waste of time"?) If even considered considered one of your revised statements startled you, even a touch bit, you purchased the factor. We aren't speaking about a few tangible commodity at the same time as we talk the time of our lives. We're speaking approximately our very lives. We no extra "have" time than we "have" inches of height.

Time isn't something extra (or less) than a way of measuring out our lives. Other cultures diploma time extraordinary approaches, and some cultures don't degree it the least bit.

Here are how a few distinctive cultures talk of time:

☐ "Think of many stuff. Do one." — Portuguese saying

☐ "Sleep quicker. We want the pillows." — Yiddish pronouncing

☐ "Haste has no blessing." —Swahili announcing

☐ "There isn't any had to seize time." — Bengali announcing

☐ "Today can't seize tomorrow."—Jamaican saying

And here's a few advice from our very very very personal famous poet, William Shakespeare, given to us from an extended-within the past era: "O, call again yesterday, bid time go returned!" "

It is not possible. The query is, virtually how "plenty" time do you "have"? In a high exceptional experience, all of us have exactly the equal "quantity," that's the triumphing instantaneous that every of us is now residing in. And this is all. And this is the important element to everything.

Even if we can't placed it away or preserve it, it does not advise we should not attempt to determine out what we will from the past and make plans for the destiny. While we're spending time collectively, we're going to have interaction in an entire lot of sports that encompass studying and planning. However, notwithstanding the fact that remembering the beyond and seeing the future are every quite innovative efforts, we aren't able to really stay in any of these worlds.

You can extraordinary live your life to the fullest within the gift second. This e-book is designed that will help you in doing so, and opposite to famous perception, you simply have an entire lot of say within the be counted. You have pretty a few leeway to choose how you want to behavior your lifestyles right now.

You must make such judgments with the help of this easy checklist, which incorporates four questions:

1. What are the vital steps?

2. Which duties have the very quality precedence and ought to be finished first?

three. What percent of it though desires to be completed?

four. How quick is it want to be completed (at the same time as is the final date)?

Your alternatives for what to do subsequent will rely upon the responses you provide to these questions. These alternatives will upload as masses as a lifestyles that is nicely lived in its whole.

Chapter 16: How Busy Would You Say You Really Are?

Are you putting in longer hours and further try than you used to within the beyond?

You spoke back inside the affirmative, right? It's proper for the awesome majority of human beings, especially people who purchase books on a manner to higher manage their time.

You have Juliet Schor's guide in this.

Schor notes in her nice-promoting ebook, The Overworked American, which she published in 1991, that the American paintings week reached its smallest difficulty in 1970, even as it turned into 39 hours, earlier than it commenced to increase. She claims that we now artwork an additional 164 hours consistent with three hundred and sixty five days, it's the equal of one complete month. She additionally discusses how, over the last area of a century, there has been a upward push in the wide variety of families with taking walks adults. There isn't always any person at home to easy, put together dinner dinner, or arrange our social lives whilst we're installing the ones longer hours at work.

She goes on to mention that the everyday American works an additional months in line with three hundred and sixty five days in assessment to maximum Europeans. For instance, the legal guidelines in Switzerland and Greece mandate that employees gather 4 weeks of excursion time in step with yr, even as the laws in France and Spain mandate that humans get preserve of five weeks. The quantity of time spent on real tour is regularly an entire lot more (five to eight weeks a 12 months in Sweden).

A studies that turned into completed now not too extended within the past via the National Sleep Foundation found that 38 percent of all complete-time employees hooked up at the least fifty hours each week at their jobs. A big kind of specialists, which encompass funding bankers, clinical residents, agency felony professionals, and lots of more, are required to art work greater than seventy hours each week, and that variety does no longer embody the papers they create domestic.

How Exactly It Is That We Are Utilizing Our Time

Our government acknowledges that we're putting in extra effort. "The commonplace extensive kind of hours labored each year by the use of personnel in the United States has increased little by little over the last numerous a few years and presently surpasses that of Japan and maximum of Western Europe," said a report that modified into published in 2004 via way of way of the National Institute for Occupational Safety and Health, that's a part of the Department of Health and Human Services.

Surprisingly, a have a have a observe achieved by way of manner of Dr. John Robinson, director of the Americans' Use of Time Project on the University of Maryland, and Dr. Geoffrey Godbey, professor of leisure studies in the College of Health and Human

Development at Penn State University, shows that the amount of free time we have is growing as nicely. Their research, which modified into blanketed in the version of Time for Life: The Surprising Ways Americans Use Their Time that turn out to be released in 1999, demonstrates that we've got got witnessed a regular upward push in the quantity of unfastened time at some stage in the route of the have a have a study's thirty-five 12 months duration. In evaluation, human beings inside the United States some of the a long time of 18 and 61 years vintage document having 40-one hours in keeping with week of free time, while in 1965, they first-class had twenty-five hours per week of free time. There come to be a large gender hollow in the amount of free time that grow to be said, with men logging 43.6 hours in keeping with week in evaluation to women's 38.Five hours. This disparity can be attributed, in big factor, to the rise in the share of on foot women who hooked up extra than twenty hours in line with week and who simultaneously commit a good sized detail in their time to home duties.

Therefore, no longer quality are we installing more hours at artwork, but we furthermore have more spare time.

Super Size My Day

How are we going as a manner to simultaneously paintings for longer hours and feature extra unfastened time? And why can we still have this experience of being rushed? According to Robinson and Godbey's studies, the same old American spends approximately 1/2 of of their enjoyment time glued to the television. It's feasible that issue spent quietly absorbing those flashing visuals might now not in a few manner check in as "entertainment," and that we unconsciously deduct that point from our loose time, the time we take into account we can pick out to spend besides we pick out out.

The quantity of time that is spent on food schooling and distinctive house duties within the United States is drastically lower as compared to what it modified into in the beyond. In addition, the time we spend seeking out services and products has reduced. Measuring Trends in Leisure: The Allocation of Time over Five Decades is a operating paper that emerge as posted in 2006 thru the Federal Reserve Bank of Boston. Mark Aguiar and Erik Hurst were the authors of this paper. They mentioned every of those findings.

We additionally spend a whole lot less time than we used to on personal care, which can be a effect of the "get dressed down" and "informal Friday" moves that received traction over the direction of the beyond decade. It might appear that the time stored via preserving off the ones sports activities has been deposited into the elegance centered for entertainment time.

However, the bulk of Americans hold to document feeling disturbing and harried.

According to a research that have become posted via way of way of the Pew Research Center in 2006, 23 percent of Americans report constantly feeling moved brief, even as some extraordinary fifty 3 percentage file occasionally feeling rushed. If we simply preserve in mind woman respondents, we find out that 26% of them normally revel in moved speedy, at the same time as fifty four% of them occasionally enjoy rushed. It must come as no wonder that the chances are notably better for operating mothers who additionally have kids in the own family. On the alternative prevent of the spectrum, virtually 7 percentage of that organization claimed that they in no manner feel moved rapid, this is a much lower percent than the tremendous forty one percentage who file commonly feeling rushed. It has come to our hobby that on foot mothers have the notion that they'll be too busy because of the fact they sincerely are too busy.

Despite the fact that the ones numbers were acknowledged to shift as an alternative over time, we may moreover moderately end that round 3-quarters of American adults revel in emotions of being harried and traumatic as a minimum part of the time.

Our jobs cause strain, and it's miles in all likelihood that they usually will: there is greater paintings to be finished than there may be time to do it, regardless of the truth that we are walking longer hours; our supervisors are pressured and bypass down their stress; industries live in flux as mergers and acquisitions live commonplace; and positions are volatile as corporations modify to changing market situations and extended foreign places competition. It have to no longer come as a surprise that chronic heartburn can also additionally forestall give up end result from the ones illnesses. Is our time even as we are not running additionally a supply of stress?

Because we are too exhausted to reflect onconsideration on some thing else to do with our time, or even if we want to, we're too sleepy to virtually do it, can we spend the maximum of our spare time inside the front of the tv? Do we have were given a lot to try this the need to set up free time undermines our pleasure of entertainment sports and drains them of any functionality restorative power they will very own? Definite opportunities. There is likewise the possibility that increasingly more us are definitely no longer capable of unwind and lighten up. We try to p.C. As loads as viable into our amusement time and produce our habit of multitasking from the place of business into our non-public lifestyles. While looking tv, we art work at the pc, even as out buying we chat on the mobile phone, and while on tour we check our e mail. There is neither a break nor a 2nd of respite available.

Logging Your Time

You are the situation of this ebook. What do you recollect that? Are you at a loss for time? Are you squandering an excessive amount of time? That is a question that can not be spoke back for you by manner of any ballot   or have a study of the way of life of the standard American. You have the energy to pick out the manner you want to spend some time and power. You are the handiest who might be in rate of figuring out how you could use that time.

First matters first, you need to take inventory of how you now spend some time. Are you prepared to take an in-intensity and sincere look at the manner you live your life, specifically how you spend it sluggish and the way you spend your days? Will you employ the findings to refocus your attention and sources in the event that you do no longer like what you find out?

It calls for artwork and a understanding of oneself to perform this intention. It is also essential to have bravery. To begin the time-logging exercise a terrific manner to ultimate for the following week, purchase a pocket e-book. Check that it's miles effects transportable and can be saved in a bag which incorporates a purse, coat pocket, backpack, or briefcase. You're going to want to have it on your person constantly. Create a list of the primary classes which you want to reveal on the very first web web page of the pocket e-book. There can be variations among your listing and mine or

every person else's.

You can also pick out out to differentiate amongst "mattress sleep" and "nap-in-the-residing-room-recliner sleep," for example, however be assured that we're capable of all encompass the identical essential instructions, together with "sleep." This portion of the hobby has the functionality to be pretty enlightening due to the fact the statistics that you accumulate right proper here might also moreover shed mild on the cause why your accomplice is generally begging you to "come to mattress."

We'll all have "eat" on our lists of vital duties that take in time, but I'll say it once more: you could preference to divide some time spent ingesting into three classes: ordinary meals which might be eaten sitting down, devour-and-run raids on nutrients at stress-through eating places, and foraging (or snacking or noshing or something you call it).

Is the time period "art work" large sufficient on your tastes? It is depending on how lots facts you want to get from your own studies. I receive as genuine with the bulk humans will want to preserve nearer tabs on precisely what we are doing at paintings, segmenting our time into categories collectively with "conferences" (likely additionally differentiating between "powerful meetings" and "general-waste- of-time conferences"?), "file writing," "responding to smartphone inquiries," "tour time" (Don't overlook travel time, which may be a high and previously overlooked time-purchaser), or maybe "ruin time

When you upload greater training, the information you acquire might be greater accurate and useful; but, it'll also become extra difficult to maintain track of. Always err on the component of overly meticulous report retaining in choice to the alternative way round when it comes to information access. The extra you decide to install, the more you can get out later. You are going to gain a good buy from the statistics which you are capable of collect at this location.

After letting some time log rest for an entire day, bypass yet again over it and make any additions or deletions which you see important. Have you neglected a few thing important? In the event that you haven't foreseen everything provided below, you're free to function topics at any time in some unspecified time in the future of the survey week. The maximum essential element is to make a listing of the property you need to hold tabs on and to test that the machine you're the usage of will will let you preserve a reasonably correct time log. (Listing hours every day as "miscellaneous" will not serve any useful purpose.)

You have become very close to being able to start your private have a observe. First matters first, jot down an estimate of the way a whole lot time you spend on every subject be counted on a weekly basis. You have the choice of calculating this based at the whole hours labored, the proportion of famous time, or every. After you are finished, you'll most in all likelihood find out that you want to transform the hours into probabilities in any case.

For instance, if you acquire as actual with which you get seven hours of sleep each night time time on common, you could located "forty nine" next to that object to your list by means of the use of way of multiplying seven thru seven. Given that there are 168 hours in each week, 40 9 hours divided with the aid of using 168 hours is 29 percentage (technically, 29.167 percentage if you need to be that real; but, "spherical 30 percent" may be extra appropriate counting on your intention).

Put down the quantity of hours and/or % that you keep in mind you want to be napping each week, and then write it down next for your estimate. If you genuinely experience that your mom have become right and that you do in fact need eight hours of sleep, then you definately ought to input "fifty six/33.Three percentage" next for your "49/29 percentage" solution. This indicates which you receive as true with that your mother come to be accurate.

Now make certain to maintain a time journal for a whole week. If there is this kind of issue as a "ordinary" week, try and pick one that does not consist of being away on vacation or on business enterprise journeys and that is, for the most detail, free from big troubles. In the event that an emergency arises during the week that you have determined on, you always have the option to begin again the following week.

It is important that you be steadfast and accurate for your actions.

Are you capable of juggle many responsibilities right now? Of path. In factor of truth, the majority of time control manuals suggest doing , three, or maybe 4 responsibilities concurrently. On the opportunity hand, for the sake of this ballot , you'll choose out the hobby that takes the lead at any given aspect in time. For instance, if you are using to art work at the identical time as moreover paying attention to an audiobook, your primary hobby is "driving to art work," and the e-book-listening is virtually incidental. If you are looking television and analyzing a e book on the same time, you want to decide whether or not or no longer you are more interested by watching television or reading the ebook.

When you first wake up on Day One, you want to get started on your log.

6:15 a.M. While laying in mattress, virtually 1/2 aware, she "listened" to the "Morning Edition."

Your subsequent notation should be made each time there's a brilliant shift on your activities.

6:32 a.M. Drove the dead frame out of the mattress. Bathroom. Shower.

Dress.

6:58 a.M. Breakfast.

The extra minute the increments, the greater correct the very last findings might be (and the more artwork the collection).

6:59 a.M. Worked sudoku puzzle.

7:02 a.M. I took a damage from operating on the sudoku problem so I must permit the dog out within the out of doors.

7:02:15 a.M. Resumed on foot sudoku puzzle.

Too unique? There's a first rate chance which you could now not find out this diploma of accuracy useful or desired. I additionally have my doubts which you would preserve recording in that manner for an entire week.

Create your notes in a layout an excellent manner to will permit you to take a look at the whole thing approximately yourself that you every need and want to recognise through the usage of the usage of the quit of the week.

Be honest, even though it hurts. People have a propensity to overestimate the amount of time they spend exercise and underestimate the amount of time they spend playing video games. You want an correct depiction of what a normal week on your lifestyles seems like for you. After then, it is as much as you to determine what, if some thing, wishes to be altered.

Although it could be hard, you should take the time to keep away from letting the act of retaining track of time have an impact on the manner you truly use that factor. If you recognize you will have to document it, you probably won't have as heaps of a desire to absolutely veg out on the couch and watch an antique episode of CSI. However, if that is what you may have finished even if you hadn't had the log, then that is what you have to do with it.

No one is needed to have a look at your mag, and you've got were given the potential to adjust some thing about your manner of lifestyles which you find objectionable (or to prefer to encompass a few component you already like, no matter what others assume, except your partner).

Make effective that you go away your self enough time on the belief of the survey week to behavior the calculations. (No, you aren't required to make a be privy to this time for your log. You are via with that.) Return to the page in which you built your listing and generated your Estimate column and your Ideal column, and enter within the figures that correspond to the Actual situation. After this factor, there need to be 3 devices of numbers after every entry.

Okay. There is a low opportunity that you may be hit with a lovely revelation. However, you could discover that estimations, beliefs, and actuals all variety by manner of a extremely good margin from each other. If so, have amusing. You are an outstanding candidate for the position of time supervisor. It's possible that in case you modify the actual times in your lifestyles to conform extra cautiously in your super, you can check a tremendous improvement inside the remarkable of your lifestyles.

It's viable that you can discover which you need to reevaluate some of your perfect instances and the reasons you chose to establish them within the first region.

If an adjustment leaps out at you presently, word it in a fourth column, "New Ideal," or "Time Management Goal":

The subsequent step is to vicinity the trade you would like to make in the shape of a statement, as follows:

"I will play video video games no a couple of and a half of hours a day," or

"I will restrict my weekly gaming time to no greater than 10 and a 1/2 of hours on common."

Congratulations. You have now completed a big first step in the direction of effective time manage. You've completed an terrific venture of keeping track of some time. You have placed maybe locations in which you may be spending too much of that time as well as areas in which you cannot be spending sufficient of that time. And you have made some early pronouncements about your destiny interests. This advanced diploma of self-attention and backbone will be fairly useful to you even if you did nothing greater to decorate your situation.

However, if you are inclined, there can be an awful lot greater that you can do to help yourself spend time wisely and well; no longer that permits you to satisfy the numbers on the chart, but as a substitute as a way to assemble a life that is both satisfied and powerful.

Be Productive

In the final bankruptcy, you have got been given commands to preserve track of the manner you commonly spend it gradual over the path of seven days. If you are thorough in completing this hobby, you need in an effort to gather an accurate and photo example of the notable classes of time use. This check is one which you may use to make ultra-modern picks concerning which pursuits deserve more of your hobby and which interests deserve less. For example, if you aren't getting as a whole lot sleep as you have to be or if looking tv is taking over extra time than you had predicted, it must be pretty glaring to you that that is the case.

But what if your sports appear to be balanced, but you continue to enjoy the burden of a packed time desk that does not let you do a whole lot? You are getting a mean of 8 hours of sleep in line with night time, balancing the amount of time you spend strolling with the quantity of time you spend playing, devoting a widespread a part of some time for your circle of relatives and friends, spending time workout and eating healthily, and doing the entirety "right," but regardless of all of your efforts, it does not seem which you are succeeding in engaging in the desires that you have set for yourself. You write down your to-do list, pass down it object via using the use of item, and bypass every one off as you finish it, however at the same time as the day is through, there are nevertheless extra topics that want to be completed. Are you operating tough however not getting anywhere? Do you enjoy like you're busy however no longer getting plenty carried out? Is it feasible that you are focusing on the "incorrect" subjects and brushing off those that are the most important?

Chapter 17: The Need For Hard Hard Paintings

The time period "busywork," which refers to sports activities that take in lots of an worker's time however don't offer a whole lot price, is kind of never covered in the mission description or taken into consideration inside the route of a standard overall overall performance evaluation. On the possibility hand, it is an hobby that many human beings interact in instead for precise obligations which might be extra excellent and giant to them. Why? It is reassuring to have a whole agenda and be not capable of tackle any greater or awesome responsibilities as a result. It makes it viable to dismiss the needs of one's coworkers with out feeling responsible and to defy the demands of 1's superiors without being afraid of being punished. Other obligations may be more tough or stressful, entail contact with strangers or awesome destructive people, encompass behaviors which can be foreign places and uncomfortable, or have an undetermined give up. All of these factors may make the jobs a whole lot less right. On the opposite hand, busywork presents some of the same advantages as profitable paintings but with out the unfavourable aspect outcomes.

People who've the fewest obligations on their plates are often the busiest people within the international. The majority of employees are beneath the impact that it's miles essential to provide their managers the effect that they are very busy, and a giant amount of managers locate it reassuring whilst their direct reviews supply the have an impact on that they'll be going for walks diligently. Nobody desires for her coworkers to get the affect that she is a "slacker," of direction.

The feeling of being green that comes from being engaged in busywork lets in us to keep away from the tension and uncertainty that consists of having our responsibilities shift. Because of the sizable false impression that interest equals productiveness, giving the affect that we are actively engaged can lie to now not simplest others but moreover ourselves. You might in all likelihood placed a number of busywork chores on your to-do listing, lease the time-saving techniques described in this ebook, and do all of your tasks in a record amount of time. But by using the use of using that point, will you have were given improved, completed your actual obligations, and visible a decrease in the tension you revel in? No. Therefore, the phrase "effective" should no longer be used as an alternative for the phrase "busy" in too many conditions.

It has been hypothesized via a number of commentators that pinnacle manipulate devised the idea of busywork to fill the time of center managers because of the shape of present day business groups. This concept has been floating approximately for a while now.

According thus far of view, middle managers have an responsibility to keep themselves occupied even as they're no longer sporting out their critical responsibility, which is to preserve an eye on the sports activities activities of decrease-degree manufacturing personnel who truely perform the undertaking. Changes in the quantity of exertions to be finished bring about slower instances, which might be the proper opportunities for managers to place roadblocks in the course of upset employees. In order to hold center managers occupied and prevent the fundamental organizational shape from breaking down, evaluations are drafted, plans are devised, systems are optimized, and vain obligations are brought to fruition.

A molehill man is a shape of busy-looking authorities who starts offevolved paintings at nine within the morning. And discovers a mountain on his artwork floor. He has until five o'clock to finish. To increase this hill to the recognition of a mountain. A expert molehill guy will often have his mountain completed via manner of lunchtime.

This vision of the con- quick commercial enterprise organisation, which can be described as pretty cynical and conspiratorial, does not constitute the strategies of present day-day organisation manage. Nevertheless, it does look like bolstered with the aid of way of the frequency with which big businesses, so you can lessen prices and enhance their bottom line, lay off a huge phase of their middle managers and keep to perform, seemingly without interruption. This is executed so you can enhance their backside line. These sports make one surprise what all of those middle managers have been doing preceding to their layoff if the organizations can get along so successfully (higher, in keeping with their press releases) after such drastic downsizing. If the businesses can get along so efficiently (better), then one has to marvel what the ones center managers have been doing.

It does not depend if busywork is an operational device created with the resource of way of better control to assist in keeping the pyramidal corporation form or a device hired by using the character to keep away from remarkable more critical duties; each manner, it lowers productiveness in direct percentage to the quantity of time that it consumes. Unfortunately, while busywork would possibly characteristic a short substitute for art work this is of more fee or is needed, it isn't always intended to replace such tough paintings. Those additional obligations will notwithstanding the truth that be there, prepared, and could very absolutely end up every greater vital and extra hard as greater time passes. Because it prevents us from focusing on different, more crucial activities, focused on lots a whole lot less valuable responsibilities may also pose a massive project to our ability to successfully manage our time. Yet we experience busy. We enjoy the strain and stress of striving to in form all of our busywork chores into their assigned time intervals, however we do not get the feeling of success that would rise up from carrying out important obligations.

Do You Admit Guilt?

How are you capable to inform in case you are engaged in art work that isn't contributing substantially to the targets of each you or the enterprise you figure for? What want to you do if the interest or undertaking that your boss has delegated to you is one which you bear in thoughts to be of little price? If it is a should, does that make it any less busywork?

Let's do not forget you experience that the challenge that changed into allocated to you via manner of your boss is an excessive amount of paintings on your liking. Let's take a step once more for a 2d and observe the quandary with an aim eye earlier than you begin acting out a state of affairs filled with righteous fury. You can be in a function to evaluate the honestly simply really worth of the undertaking, however it is also viable that you do not have all the information you want to assess the bigger image. It's viable that the outcomes of this venture are at the critical direction for a person else in the organisation which you aren't acquainted with. In spite of the reality that it is able to appear like vain busywork, and however the fact that resisting it would require pretty a few time and effort on your component, the challenge in query sincerely wishes to be completed. Ensure which you have a clear facts of what is important (and what isn't always), spend really the minimal amount of time working on it, and then move directly to a few factor else.

In well-known, the time period "busywork" refers to a preference that need to be made, as does the terrible cease result of busywork. If we choose to avoid greater sizable, intention-associated, and potentially hard assignments by means of the use of the use of losing time on topics that might not rely after they'll be executed, then we're responsible of doing busywork. This is due to the fact we are responsible of selecting to avoid greater hard obligations. Or, if the amount of strive that we placed into a piece is greater than what is required folks. If the report is an internal record and the readers may be worried most effective with its content material cloth material, then the attempt of internet page beautification is not realistic busywork. It is possible to spend hundreds of time perfecting the advent of a document through selecting fonts, laying out pages artistically, and using images. You have made the choice to spend some time on components which may be beside the factor to the art work handy and haven't any relating to its final results.

Therefore, fee is crucial to the concept of busywork, and charge is an problem of opinion. Whoever is making the choice has a big impact. We have confirmed that a manager's judgment can be given more weight than that of her employees in terms of judging the importance of a assignment, and an inexpensive employee is willing to without a doubt accept the truth that that is the case. However, in many situations, you're the quality who receives to assess the importance of a chunk, choose how lots effort to invest in it, after which experience the cease end result of your hard work after it's far over. It is vital that we get the preliminary step proper, that's making the proper choice after carefully weighing the professionals and cons of what we are doing.

Avoiding Busywork

The massive majority human beings are able to protect our movements whilst pressed, ought to that be critical. Even if the sports which is probably now occupying our time are not on a key path interior our most crucial venture, we can also notwithstanding the truth that find out sufficient motives to preserve doing those sports on the way to sate our very personal desires and be content material fabric with our preference. Usually. After all, we're specialists, and as such, we are extra familiar than anybody else with the necessities which is probably associated with our art work.

However, the essential element to converting our conduct—to forestall losing time on busywork and begin spending time on extra important obligations—is to apprehend our weaknesses in choice to shield them. This is the first step inside the system of changing how we spend our time. Our shortcomings, at least on this particular example, encompass an incapacity to surely recognize our desires, to convert those objectives into tasks, and to prioritize those sports activities in a way that is steady with accomplishing the goals. This is easy to recognize and trust in precept, however setting it into movement is a miles extra difficult corporation.

This is because of the truth that our schedules being disrupted via the usage of special needs, therefore rendering our plans vain. There are calls that want to be back, e-mails that want to be treated, requests from coworkers that want to be addressed, and little or huge fires that want to be placed out, counting on what degree our responsibilities are in. It is possible for us to be well on our way to completing notable artwork at the same time as we are suddenly confronted thru trivial issues and inconsequential duties. As a end end result, via the stop of the day, we might also enjoy exhausted but upset with the eight hours of frenetic hobby that we've had been given truly completed.

If busywork is the supply of the problem, then removing it want to bring about an boom in productiveness, right? Certainly not in each case. It is possible that we are preoccupied with meaningless sports activities because of the reality we are not able or unwilling to finish huge duties. And even though we do no longer have busywork to distract us, we're able to no matter the reality that be no longer capable to complete large sports for numerous motives. In this situation, the issue handy might be now not the quantity of busywork, however as a substitute every distinctive hassle altogether.

To maintain to engage in low-fee sports activities, instead, makes it extra tough for us to perform giant obligations. This is an similarly valid thing. As changed into indicated in advance than, step one is to decide what our goals are in order that we are able to realize and put together the activities on the manner to purpose our achievement in achieving the ones desires. Therefore, we want to direct our interest on completing the ones jobs as opposed to any of the others. Isn't it easy lessen? Of course now not! If this were the case, there wouldn't be nearly as many courses, which encompass books, mag articles, and workshops, dedicated to supporting individuals who feel helpless because of the truth they'll be not capable of arrange their time efficaciously.

]

Chapter 18: Managing Time

In current society, effective time manage is taken into consideration a non-public remember in preference to a communal one. If you are too busy and below too much stress, that's your own fault. If you are able to, see to its decision.

Just ensure which you are on time for artwork and which you pay all your payments on time.

But earlier than we get all of the manner proper right down to the company of making splendid changes for your existence, permit's take a step again and recall the bigger image of society.

Could we, as a society, institute a piece schedule that includes a six-hour artwork day, a thirty-hour artwork week, and a paid excursion for all employees?

Would or not it's miles feasible for us to manual the implementation of possibility running arrangements which includes mission sharing and bendy scheduling everywhere?

Shouldn't we understand "workaholic" for what it definitely is—a vital social illness—in desire to treating it like a medal of honor?

In the event that this isn't the case, are we ready to bear in mind the actual rate that our society incurs for health care, in addition to underemployment and unemployment?

Are You Capable of Change?

It isn't always truely not possible. In the Fifties, we made the selection that thwarting the possibility of a Communist takeover need to be our top assignment, and as a cease result, we surely reorganized society to advantage this intention. (One vital purpose President Eisenhower created the Interstate Highway System, for instance, became as a technique of evacuating our towns in the event of a nuclear attack.) And inside the early 1960s, John F. Kennedy pledged that america may additionally have a person at the moon inside the decade, and we had been a achievement in carrying out this purpose.

Examine the approaches wherein people's perspectives on smoking cigarettes have changed over the last 20 years for the duration of society. That did now not simply take region. The people positioned forth some of attempt to modify their mindsets.

There is functionality for vast shifts inside the social focus and ideals of people. But in the interim, awareness on the one detail of society which you have control over: yourself.

What precisely are your alternatives as regards to the restricted amount of time?

Many humans get the impact that some hassle or all of our lives are spinning out of our manipulate. Because it is this sort of popular prevalence, the sentiment has been increased to the recognition of a life-style and is now being targeted thru classified ads. Advertisers are a fulfillment in promoting devices thru connecting with the emotions of customers and tailoring their objects and services to the possibilities of the clients' lives. They aren't suggesting that we want to have the sensation that we're powerless. They are working on the idea that we do, and they're providing what they be given as actual with to be a partial solution, a time saver, an island of calm inside the midst of an ocean of turmoil, and one incredible product that capabilities because it must.

It should not come as a wonder that the advertising and advertising and marketing international is at once to us; with their research, questionnaires, and awareness organizations, they may be constantly cutting and dicing our sporting events and alternatives into smaller and further digestible components. They are conscious, as an example, that there were 126 billion "on-the-bypass eating occasions" within the United States in the yr 2005. That's more than one constant with individual every day for every men, female, and youngster, it sincerely is an excessive amount of snacking. Food makers are keen to offer the gas (check: snack meals) that feeds our power to indulge and permits preserve us on the circulate because of this information, which has energized the food producers. The fashionable monetary fee of all of these conveniences is predicted to be $63 billion in step with yr.

The food region, which modified into answerable for perfecting the drive-through enjoy, is answerable for training us a manner to consume at the same time as the use of, that is a appreciably essential multitasking ability within the present day world. The majority of agencies that sell devices and services also embody time-saving and available abilties into their items and services, and they highlight those competencies in their advertising and advertising and marketing and marketing efforts. This is the muse upon which the laptop hardware and software program software groups were normal, and that they function shining examples of the way productiveness can be prolonged. Despite this, the need to better arrange one's schedule is this type of pervasive issue that it has delivered about the development of products which encompass apparel that calls for minimal upkeep, appliances that lessen the quantity of manual difficult work required, digital toll lanes, and precise expedient solutions for every side of our lives. Our manner of life has vastly advanced because of technological improvements which encompass self-parking motors, the ability to hire a person to wait in line on our behalf, and the usage of mobile gadgets to find public restrooms in surprising cities.

We receive as actual with that the reality that some of those devices assist to isolate us from our environment and get rid of the need of engaging in social interplay are more advantages of using those topics. We need a plethora of equipment to brief prepare us for paintings and existence, further to to proper away discover answers to any issues which could come up. Whereas the woodsman of yesteryear required a dependable knife for dealing with his surroundings, we require a plethora of devices. When we are too busy, we buy a products or services which will help us get through the state of affairs each physically and mentally. This is our approach of "shopping for our way out."

The money and time spent shopping for, the growing dependence, and the lost pleasures of getting prepared, smelling, and savoring (and, in masses of instances, chewing) one's personal food are all subjects that must be factored into the entire fee of such conveniences. However, we want to additionally endure in mind the real fee of such conveniences. When we push ourselves to paintings ever more difficult, ever quicker, and ever longer, we want to keep in mind the toll that this takes on our our our our bodies, which embody our eyes, our stomachs, and our minds.

When you first start keeping accurate score, you can find which you need to regulate a number of the alternatives you're making in reaction to this.

Challenges Presented by the Conventional Method of Time Management

In the object that is published within the tabloid newspaper, it's far added that with the useful useful resource of following the advice of a time management professional, a person may additionally earn greater minutes or maybe hours on a each day basis. (You recognize the sort of newspaper I'm speakme about, the type that nobody reads, an awful lot on my own purchases, however that though claims a paid readership within the hundreds of hundreds.)

One of these useful pointers comes from Lucy Hedrick, the author of 365 Ways to Save Time, and it is as follows:

"If you do no longer have time to take a look at, letter-write, cook dinner, or exercise, wake up in advance within the morning."

"If you do now not have time to examine, letter-write, prepare dinner, or workout."

It seems that many people find out fulfillment with this method of time manage. According to the findings of various professionals, folks who specialize in the have a study of sleep, the not unusual quantity of sleep that Americans gather each night time time has decreased thru sixty to ninety mins in evaluation to the quantity of sleep they received 10 to 15 years in the beyond. Not simplest does she advise sleeping fewer hours, but she additionally believes that you need to. . . "Make certain that your breakfast is short and easy. Make your self a "blender breakfast" with a banana, a few fruit juice, some granola, and a dash of honey. " And, "Try a smoothie for lunch."

"If your bathtub needs to be wiped clean, you need to do it at the same time as you're inside the bathe." You may additionally additionally furthermore exfoliate as quick as you're completed washing your hair or while the conditioner is doing its technique."

You have the ability to perform such obligations. It is feasible a great way to put together a huge pitcher of "blender breakfast," positioned it in a cooler, and save it to your vehicle so that you can also drink it on the manner to paintings.

In order to be aware of a self-help software at the same time as you are cleaning the grout within the shower together together with your toothbrush and rinsing the shampoo from your hair, you'll probable convey a CD participant this is water-proof into the bathroom with you and use it there. You need to even placed on your clothes into the bathe, much like the protagonist in Anne Tyler's novel The Accidental Tourist, so you can also need to clean your duds at the same time as you grouted, listened, and showered on the equal time. This might in all likelihood allow you to wash your garments even as you showered, which might will will let you preserve time.

It's possible that those strategies may work quite for some human beings, however others will discover that the fee they pay to shop a few seconds is actually too steep.

It's viable that you can want to bite your meal a good way to affirm which you've without a doubt consumed something. If that is the case, you will need to get hold of the pain of the situation further to the unstoppable march of time as you munch on your Grape Nuts.

Even on the busiest of days, you may find out that a three-minute secure haven inside the form of a scorching heat bathe is truely what your frame and thoughts are craving to get the day started out off on the proper foot.

Some human beings, on the other hand, are the kind who upward thrust early and exercise consultation for 40-five to 90 mins on a every day foundation. This is done in advance than they gnaw their way thru breakfast after which soak in a steamy bathe. That appears to be strolling for them. It's feasible that it can not be simply proper for you.

When we pass for a jog, a number of us need to pay attention to music, while others want to certainly permit their mind wander. You would possibly in all likelihood experience a beautiful multitasking second thru attaching a speakerphone on your treadmill when you have been so willing to make the maximum of your run. This may want to allow you to educate each your body and your mind on the equal time, which is probably beneficial to each.

There need to be a place for everything and the whole thing need to be in its location, which incorporates having tidy files, a easy laptop, and a ground that you can sincerely stroll on. Some of you need to impose inflexible order on your workspace. Others be part of the "compost heap" faculty of laptop manipulate and are pretty content material fabric to jump over the plenty of files, books, and magazines that in the end accumulate at the ground.

Even with the sloppy place of work, I changed into able to get a few assist. Dru Scott, in her e-book How to Put More Time in Your Life, praises "the hidden delights" of clutter. She refers to folks which are disorganized as "divergent thinkers," a phrase that, you need to agree, sounds far extra attractive than "messy slob."

The argument is that the traditional recommendations for effective time management aren't relevant to each person. You are answerable for charting your very very own path via the cautioned bodily games and sports activities which may be provided right proper right here. You won't want to exert manipulate over a few elements of your existence, even in case you are capable of doing so.

The site visitors is only one example of the various elements that none parents have manipulate over. It is extraordinary that you can get stopped in web page site visitors in case you are in the again of the wheel of a car in any part of the sector this is more densely populated than the outback of Australia. Control the go with the flow of vehicular web page site visitors? It couldn't harm to take the time to steer in opposition to the glide of the river in that you are swimming.

If you time table an appointment, you need to assume that someone will preserve you geared up. Your night meal can be disrupted by using the usage of a salesclerk calling on the cellphone. Your manager goes available you an unanticipated challenge on the 11th hour. Your child will get ill at the day that you are scheduled to provide that massive presentation in the the front of the board. It is inevitable. The best difficulty you can do is try and anticipate what is going to arise and react therefore.

Oh, So That's Where All of Our Time Actually Goes!

The following bleak state of affairs is the same old of dwelling that may be predicted inside the United States, ordinary with performance expert Michael Fortino. During the course of your life, you will spend:

☐ seven years spent cleansing the relaxation room, six years spent consuming food,

☐ Five years were spent in line, three years were spent in conferences, and 5 years had been spent

☐ Two years have been spent playing cellular smartphone tag, eight months were spent studying unsolicited mail, and the remaining six months were spent idling at pink lighting fixtures.

And on a regular day, you may be interrupted seventy-3 times, deliver an hour's without a doubt well really worth of hard work home with you, take a look at for much less than 5 minutes, talk collectively along with your partner for 4 minutes, exercise consultation for fewer than three minutes, and have interaction in little one-associated sports for simply minutes.

Nightmarish. Do you want to alter that photo? It isn't always too past due if you need to reorient your existence; just as it have turn out to be no longer too past due for terrible Scrooge, who become stunned into lifestyles exchange through the ghosts of Christmas beyond, present, and future, it is not too late for you. In the give up, that is what powerful time control comes right proper right down to.

No consider what you do, despite the fact that, the truth remains that you will must spend a large amount of time equipped in line, idling at purple lighting, and kicking your ft up in equipped rooms.

Some Initial Changes To Get Control Of Your Time

You also can make big-scale adjustments. You may additionally need to p.C. Up your house, say good-bye to your own family, and visit a far off cabin inside the Dakotas to pursue a profession as a landscape painter. You ought to. You likely might not, but, and also you in all likelihood ought to not each.

You are able to make inconsequential modifications with out the help or authorization of anybody else. You may, as an example, teach yourself to take 4 brief breaks each day, or you could put into effect any of the alternative suggestions that I will offer in a later economic disaster.

As you are making your way thru this ebook, deliver yourself permission to analyze as many tremendous options as you in all likelihood can. Some of them might not make a whole lot sense. You won't have achievement with a number of them. There is probably some which can be from your fee variety for a number of specific reasons. However, in case you positioned your creativeness, strive, and electricity into this research, you will find out strategies to make adjustments which may be vast and lifestyles-placing forward for you.